Since October 1966 when PERSONA opened to overwhelming critical acclaim, the names of Ingmar Bergman and Liv Ullman have been synonymous with outstanding cinema artistry. Discovered by Bergman, already a highly respected film and stage director, while a fledgling actress with the Norwegian National Theater, Ullman was recognized almost immediately as a performer of international stature for her sensitive portrayal in the stunning PERSONA. She had become more than just his protegee, for shortly after the completion of the filming, Ullman, while married to another man, bore Bergman, also married, a child, and for five years lived with him in the face of scandal on the desolate island of Faro.

LIV ULLMANN & IngmarBergman

BERNIE GARFINKEL

A BERKLEY MEDALLION BOOK
published by
BERKLEY PUBLISHING CORPORATION

Contents

LIV ULLMANN
&
Ingmar Bergman

CHAPTER ONE

Myths and Masks

The first scene, "Innocence and Panic," from Scenes from a Marriage: *Marianne and Johan are being interviewed by a reporter from a women's magazine for a series on happily married couples.*

Marianne: So we started living together. Our mothers never batted an eye, though we thought they'd be terribly shocked. Not at all! In fact, they became good friends. Suddenly we were accepted as Johan and Marianne. After six months we got married.
Johan: Besides, by then we were in love.
Marianne: Terribly.

Johan: We were considered an ideal married couple.
Marianne: And so it has gone on.
Mrs. Palm: No complications?
Marianne: We've had no material worries. We're on good terms with friends and relations on both sides. We have good jobs that we both like. We're healthy.
Johan: And so on and on, to an almost vulgar degree. Security, order, comfort, and loyalty. It all has a suspiciously successful look.
Marianne: Naturally, like other people, we have our differences. That goes without saying. But we agree on all the important things.

The interviewer has the chirpy, syrupy self-confidence of someone who is always intruding on other people's lives. For this regular feature in her magazine, she always asks the same questions. Are you happy? What is love? Do you ever quarrel? And she sits back waiting for the answers. Her readers believe in "romantic love," and this is what she wants to hear about. But from past experience, she knows that no matter how much "in love" the couple may say they are, at some point in the interview the discords, small or large, will surface. In this case, Johan and Marianne are unwavering in their portrait of happiness. "It sounds fantastic," she says of their marriage, still hoping the burnt toast will pop up. But Johan and Marianne have no problems. In fact, says Johan, perhaps they should consider the fact that "the very lack of problems" is a problem.

And so photographs are taken and the interview ends. Johan and Marianne are complacently secure and satisfied in their present and trusting in their future, seemingly unable to imagine that the sweet reasonableness of their life could ever turn sour. They agree on "all the important things," says Marianne. In fact, of course, they never talk about what are the truly important things to each of them; so it's no problem to maintain the facade of agreement.

Watching this scene, we get the feeling that there's plenty wrong here, but of course we don't yet know just what or why. There are clues in Marianne's and Johan's speeches. Johan admits that he fears the future. He says, sounding fatuously secure, that even if it makes him seem conceited, he must admit that he is intelligent, successful, well balanced, cultivated, popular, a good mixer, and sexy. But when he declares that he is a splendid lover, he turns immediately to Marianne to get her confirmation. "Aren't I?" he asks, which is like asking your mother if she loves you. For her part, Marianne will talk about love only reluctantly, and then she admits that "No one has told me what love is. And I'm not even sure it's necessary to know." "Anyway," she says, "if you have comradeship and tolerance and a sense of humor, love is not so important."

But certainly these tiny gristles, as it seems, are not enough to stop the interviewer from serving up her romantic stew. "Two young people," she writes, "strong, happy, with a constructive attitude toward life in general, but who have never forgotten all the same to give love first place." Johan reads the article to a couple who are their best friends at a dinner party in Johan and Marianne's apartment. Marianne is glowingly beautiful in the candlelight. She has her "company face" on; she seems more vibrant, more physically alive by far than she did when she was talking to the interviewer. She is so much more her own person presiding at the table in front of guests that we flash back to a remembrance of her in the first scene and get a further clue to the state of affairs in this marriage. She has lost some of her reserve, she is not so tentative nor schoolgirlish (at thirty-five) as she seemed to be in front of Mrs. Palm. She does not defer quite so obviously to

Johan, and she seems larger physically. Perhaps most revealing, her bright blue eyes seem open and unveiled, and we remember that in the first scene, her eyes were shadowed; they seemed to mask a question of her own that she never got to ask. It is the contrast of her brighter, company self that bring these intimations of unquiet so clearly out into the open, so that they are like highway signs that flashed by too quickly to be read at the time, but now, miles later, we suddenly realize, signaled danger ahead, scenes from an unhappy marriage.

Max Von Sydow, who has appeared with Liv Ullmann in four of the six movies she has made under Ingmar Bergman's direction, says of her: "She has a rare ability to express emotions in front of a camera in a very pure way, very directly. It is something I have rarely seen." Von Sydow said that after they had made *Shame* together in 1967. Under Bergman's guidance, Ullmann's capacity to register nuances of emotion in front of a camera has flowered enormously since then, and in *Scenes from a Marriage*, her control and virtuosity in this regard are nothing less than astounding. And as the film progresses, she presents us with the portrait of a woman so fully realized, so *real*, that we almost hold our breath waiting for the next word, gesture, expression, as if we were living her experiences with her instead of merely (but not merely) watching her act. So real is she, so fully orchestrated in expressiveness and emotion, that she carries the film onto a higher level of existence, transforming it from being an extremely well made and well acted one into a work of art that exists beyond its story and content— which in themselves are overwhelmingly powerful—as a *Mona Lisa*, a definitive exposition of the life of this woman named Marianne.

At any given moment in the film, Liv Ullmann is

there in such full-blown reality, living Marianne's life on screen in such depth and dimension, that it might well be called *Scenes from Marianne's Life*. One can think of few actresses—living or dead—who could approach this level of playing, and, as is always the case with a work of art—which becomes one because nothing need be added, nothing should be subtracted—no one who could fulfill the role as perfectly. There are, of course, other actresses who would have made Marianne alive and real, if a different person, but having seen Ullmann do her, we are totally satisfied and can't imagine—nor do we want to imagine—anyone else in the role.

Before *Scenes from a Marriage* was released around the world, after having been made for and shown on Swedish television, Liv Ullmann was known to most movie fans as a highly superior Scandinavian actress who had appeared in a number of Bergman films and received high praise in them. She had also, like Ingrid Bergman two decades previously, endured the scorn of Scandinavian moralists by falling in love with her director, as Bergman had with the Italian Roberto Rossellini, and bearing his child out of wedlock. In 1972 Liv Ullmann's fame reached as far as Hollywood, and the moguls there, always hungry for new goddesses, decided that she should be the newest. She came to Los Angeles to promote *The Emigrants*, a film she had made with the Swedish director Jan Troell, and, very quickly, she was signed up to do two American films, a musical remake of *Lost Horizon*, directed by Blake Edwards, and the film version of the Broadway play, *Forty Carats*, directed by Milton Katselas.

In *Lost Horizon* she would play Catherine, the charming school-mistress in Shangri-La, singing and dancing for the first time in a film. In *Forty Carats* she would play a forty-year-old woman in love with a twenty-one-year-old boy. The roles were departures for her, as was making movies in Hollywood, and she looked on the whole prospect as "fun."

Destined in Hollywood's judgment to follow in the footsteps of Garbo and Bergman, Liv was given the big buildup, which began as soon as *Lost Horizon* went into production. A *Time* magazine cover story at the end of 1972 called her "an ordinary, extraordinary woman," and predicted that "a new star is about to burst onto U. S. movie screens." But between the lines, even *Time* had some reluctance in transforming the "art-house actress" and "specialist in gloomy Nordic agonies" into a Hollywood-style starlet of thirty-three. And, as it turned out, *Time*'s doubts were justified. *Lost Horizon*, in which Liv shared star billing with Peter Finch, Charles Boyer, John Gielgud and Michael York, was flat and unexciting, and the general critical response was that she didn't really come across in the role. As for *Forty Carats*, despite the enthusiasm of Mike Frankovich, the producer, and Leonard Gershe, the author, who rewrote the role better to fit her, Liv turned out not to fit it at all. Though Warner Brothers went ahead with its production of *The Abdication*, in which she played opposite Peter Finch in the role of Queen Christina of Sweden that Garbo had once played (probably a key element in the studio's choice— "it's gotta make her the new Garbo, right?") it was obvious that, whatever else Liv Ullmann might be, she was not a goddess in the old Grauman Chinese Theater mold.

Since she did not care for the artificiality and luxury of life in Beverly Hills as a long-term proposition, Liv was content to return to Sweden after *Forty Carats* was finished shooting, particularly since she began work immediately on *Scenes from a Marriage*. Her Hollywood sojourn had a significance beyond the surface story of wrong projects and failed films. She was not the first actress to go West with high hopes and great talents and, despite all the power of Hollywood's money and promotional apparatus, fall flat. A film project is, after all, a complicated endeavor, subject to the control of a sometimes ill-assorted board of directors that includes the writer, producer, director, studio head, and wife of the conglomerate's chairman in New York.

But the bandwagon psychology that afflicts Hollywood (as in repeating Ullmann in Garbo's role in *The Abdication*) was never more apparent than in the casting of Liv Ullmann in the role of the forty-year-old real estate agent from New York (but Scandinavian-born) who becomes irresistibly attractive to Edward Albert (son of Eddie Albert), a twenty-one-year-old American zooming around a Greek island on a motorcycle when he meets her. The problem was not with her age (she was thirty-two when she did the film) though she was unhappy with the way in which she was made to look older in it. And the problem was not with the good intentions of Gershe and Frankovich, both of whom were sincerely counting on her talents as an actress to carry her through. They were counting also, no doubt, on the firepower of Hollywood publicity to light up the sky with her image as the new bombshell from Scandinavia who would step up to the royal box of the previous Scandinavian film queens, Garbo and Bergman.

What they overlooked completely is the essence of Liv Ullmann and why she is a great actress. From the moment she and Edward Albert meet in *Forty Carats* after her car has broken down on the Greek island, it is obvious that there is a gap between them no spark of Ullmann's talent can ever jump. She is far too dignified and sensible, far too intelligent and probing, far too aware of the complexities of life and far too sexually mature, to consider for a moment an alliance with the kind of twenty-one-year-old man she is supposed to love in the film. He is full of the boyish, assumed but-not-yet-learned, prowess at being a man that twenty-one-year-olds adopt until the real thing comes along. He is so transparently playing at being "mature" that a woman-actress who is Liv Ullmann couldn't possibly accept him as the real thing unless she had some weird mother complex. At the heart of what must be her rejection of him as a suitor, her inability to *take him seriously*, is the precise kind of sexuality she projects as a woman. It is the exact opposite of Mrs. Robinson's sexual itch for the graduate, which is a circumstantial, hot-pants, do-something-for-my-boredom letch for a young body.

The forty-year-old woman in *Forty Carats* has gone beyond this; her sexuality is not a whim that she wants to satisfy as she would a taste for ice cream; it is part of her totality as a woman and its object clearly must be a man who communicates to her as a person. In short, there is no way we can believe that she will develop a passionate desire for the callow, confused (beneath his surface assurance) young man whose personality is as thin as a dime.

What is fascinating in all this is the fact that, even in the writing of the film, no effort is made to bridge this gap. Despite the clear evidence that this man and woman can't be attracted to each other as the film is written—a conclusion that must have been obvious from the first rushes—the two characters continue to be their nonattracting selves, two parallel lines that can't ever meet for the hour and twenty minutes of the charade. So the initial problem, which is that Liv Ullmann is not the right kind of woman for the part, is totally ignored in the script, and no effort is made to make her part more amenable to her personality.

Such is Hollywood. Such is not Ingmar Bergman's film "company," which consists of some twenty actors, actresses and technicians who have made dozens of films with Bergman, always under his sole control. As part of this group, Liv Ullmann has made seven movies with Bergman. The impression one might get from *Forty Carats*—that somehow she is limited as an actress, is incapable of playing a frivolous or sexy woman—is immediately dispelled by watching her in such films as *Persona, Hour of the Wolf, The Passion of Anna, Cries and Whispers* and, of course, *Scenes from a Marriage.* Certainly, her roles in these films have been "serious and dramatic." But in them, and in numerous stage productions from Ibsen's *A Doll's House* to Bertolt Brecht's *Mother Courage*, she has exhibited an enormous range, brilliant virtuosity and control. Bergman himself believes that she can play comedy, as she does, too.

It was unfortunate that *Forty Carats* was the vehicle she chose for her first exposure in a light and sophisticated role, since neither scriptwriter nor director was tuned in to the kind of person she is, which in her case, means the kind of actress she is—one whose perception, intelligence, and craft can respond to a role that represents a person who is real and dimensional. This does not mean at all that this person has no relation to the fantasy world that blooms in dreams, madness or simply wayward behavior. On the contrary, many of the roles she has played for Bergman have been anchored in the world of the imagination and the subconscious that Bergman probes. In a romantic comedy like *Forty Carats*, however, as in any story, the minimum requirement is a character who makes us believe he or she truly *exists,* has perceptions and emotions that engage our interest. With its typical obtuseness, Hollywood was unable to supply this character, someone real enough to engage Liv Ullmann's superior talents.

All my life, I've tried to be an eight-by-ten glossy. I try to give the effect that everything's perfect and that star ladies don't ever go to the bathroom and the hair and

9

the eyelashes are always in place and the shoes and jewelry are eternally perfect because people want to believe that of star ladies.

——Ann Miller in a 1975 interview
in *Esquire* magazine.

Hooray for Hollywood, hooray for fantasy land. In this same interview, Ann Miller told about her early days at MGM: "Mr. Mayer told the press department that I was to be given star treatment . . . they'd choose a boyfriend to take me to the premiere of a new film. It looked good in print, but it was all manufactured—Donna Reed, Ava Gardner, Junie Allyson—for all of us. They'd choose our dresses and hats and feathers so we'd look pretty. The furs and cars were always rented. You were Cinderella and nothing was really real."

That was the stuff of which the stories in fan magazines were made. Times have changed, of course, and no one today believes the stories in fan magazines—do they? The magazines still exist and still tell their readers how the stars "really" live and love. The difference between the stories now and those that ran in Hollywood's heyday is that yesterday's described the furniture in a bedroom, today's the latest abortion. The shock content has reached a far higher level, but today's stories are as likely to be as phony and manufactured as the dream life churned out by the publicity departments in the good old days.

On the whole, it's probably true that more truth gets printed about actors today than twenty-five years ago. But the point is, as Liv Ullmann's experience in Hollywood indicated, that publicity is still often considered to be a substitute for the content and quality of a movie. And, unfortunately, it often is, so that a bad movie becomes inordinately successful. And because publicity still works, the feeling that an actor's (not to mention a politican's) "image" can be created and manipulated for profit is still very strong in America.

This concept is foreign to Liv Ullmann for a couple of reasons. One is that the Scandinavian film industry is small, and the few home-grown films generally achieve satisfactory distribution and find a strong audience if they are at all worthwhile—without elaborate, gimcrack publicity campaigns. And the second is that, as a person, the whole concept of image is repugnant to her. It is, in fact, the exact opposite of what she has attempted to do in both her private life and her career as an actress. Her technique in her roles is utterly naturalistic, based on the feeling that the most powerful and pure emotion develops from the least obvious effects. What she is after, in essence, is honesty. "I think we should dare to show what's inside us," she says. "I think the problem with the world today is that we are having masks, we are guarding ourselves, we are so afraid of being 'dumb' and everything with each other. . . . The camera lets me be honest, and come out with things that maybe I wouldn't do."

In her personal life as well, she feels that she has changed enormously as the result of her experiences, and a chief element in the change has been her efforts to present herself more honestly to herself and to others. "I discovered that I had been brought up to be the sort of person people wanted me to be, so that they would like me and I would not be uncomfortable for them. That person wasn't me at all. . . . When I started to be me, I felt I had more to give. I found it more interesting to live."

It is this honesty that shines through in her portrayal of Marianne in *Scenes* and makes her impact in the role so strong. Audiences recognize it and love it because it's so rare. And yet, of course, it would be foolish to think that Liv Ullmann is Marianne. This is not the "honesty" of the talk-show guest, whose "confessions" are often as contrived as one of Louis B. Mayer's premieres, nor is it the undisciplined and compulsive outpourings of a patient to his analyst. It's the artistic honesty of intelligence, intuition, and craft working together to create a real person out of a character in a script.

The resources to create characters who "live" come from an actor's own experiences and convictions as well as his training and talent. In Liv Ullmann's case, she has consciously tried to explore herself as a person with her function as an actress in mind. And in doing so, she has come to believe that her path is to meet life head-on, to strike out and struggle to discover who she is and how she should arrange her life as a result of this knowledge. At the opposite end of the scale, and far more common, is the actor who takes on in real life at least some of the characteristics of the roles he's played, and feeds them back with tricks and techniques to go on in new roles defining the same person over and over again.

It was her sense of honesty and concern for "reality" that made Liv Ullmann uncomfortable in Hollywood. "If I lived here all my life," she confessed, "I'd be continually embarrassed by this big house, the luxurious cars and everything else. Nobody has these things in Norway." Beyond that, she found "so little communication there," and, again, an artificiality that she hated: "You couldn't even see the toilets," she said, "because they were discreetly disguised as chairs."

Her commitment to honesty in life was demonstrated publicly and rather embarrassingly when she was in New York for a six-week engagement in Joseph Papp's New York Shakespeare Festival production of *A Doll's House* at Lincoln Center. The contretemps was quite silly but revealing nevertheless. It revolved around a party given by Andrew Stein, a New York State legislator, in honor of Shirley MacLaine's newly released film, *The Other Half of the Sky, A China Memoir*, and her just-published book, "*You Can Get There from Here*. Stein sent out invitations which said: "Liv Ulman [sic] and Andrew Stein would like to have you join them at a party..." to be held at Stein's father's Park Avenue apartment.

A week or so before the invitations went out, Liv and Stein were mentioned in at least one gossip column as having a romance. After denying to one columnist that there was any romance, Liv learned that Stein had sent the invitations with her name on them to around one hundred invited guests prominent in show business, politics, and journalism, among them Paul Newman and Joanne Woodward, the Robert Redfords, Gloria Steinem, and Elia Kazan. She thereupon wrote a note to all the invitees, saying: "I am mildly surprised that Andrew Stein wants to share hosting a party with me. If he had taken the trouble to ask me before he sent out the invitations with my name on them, or known me better than he does by having met me once at a dinner party, he would have known that I am much too shy to host a party for so many people, most of whom I have never met...."

To Liv Ullmann, the embarrassment of admitting shyness to begin with, and of having publicly to air a quarrelsome situation, was overshadowed by her refusal to do something she didn't want to do, something she would have to "fake" if she did it. It seems safe to say that, faced with the chance to meet a good many well-known people and to be part of one of today's "media events," another person in her place would have gone along instead of being painfully honest in setting the record straight.

The New York production of *A Doll's House* was sold out two weeks before the play opened. The reason was, quite simply, Liv Ullmann's appearance in the play; rather than the feeling that this would be a definitive production of a work that's been done and done. So, finally, more than two years after her *Time* magazine cover, Liv Ullmann had achieved the recognition (or stardom, as Hollywood would say) in America that Hollywood foresaw for her.

How this happened was interesting. It did not come about through her American movies such as *Forty Carats*, *The Abdication*, and *Lost Horizon*, all of which were decidedly unsuccessful and showed her to poor advantage besides. (Woody Allen remarked: "If I had my life to live over, I would do everything the same—except see the remake of *Lost Horizon*.") Until *Cries and Whispers* (1973) and *Scenes from a Marriage*, her Bergman films, such as *Persona*, *Shame*, and *The Passion of Anna*, had limited popular appeal. And even *The Emigrants* and *The New Land* (directed by the Swedish Jan Troell), which were critical successes, were not widely popular successes. *Cries and Whispers* was the first Bergman film that began to reach out to a popular audience in America. It won an Oscar as the best foreign film, which Liv accepted for Bergman at the Academy Award ceremonies. (She had herself received the prestigious New York Film Critics Award as best actress for her role in it.)

But the passionate intensity of the expectation induced by her appearance in *A Doll's House* could be traced directly to *Scenes from a Marriage*, which, for a number of reasons, transformed her in the eyes of the American public from being just "a very fine Swedish actress" into something approaching a cult figure, admired for her acting to begin with, but admired as well for being the kind of person, and more important-ly, the kind of woman she was perceived to be. This was a woman of accomplishment and talent, beauty and independence, and, gloriously, in an era of women's liberation that began more than one hundred years ago but achieved success only in the last ten, a liberated women who seemed capable of muting if not erasing completely all of the hostility and abrasion that the change in women's status was inducing between men and women today.

The way she was perceived by both men and women resulted, fascinatingly, as in the case of most popular heroes, from a classic mixture of fact and myth. The facts came from the events and circumstances of her life. The myth came from the role she played in *Scenes from a Marriage*, which was a powerful examination in itself of what women's liberation may be all about. As had happened before and will happen again, the perfection of her playing in the film led her audience to confuse her film self with her real self. Vivien Leigh suffered the same fate in the public mind, which identified her as the kind of woman that the character of Scarlett O'Hara made her seem to be in *Gone with the Wind*.

In fact, for once, the public was not wrong in its myth-making. Liv Ullmann is very much the person she is conceived to be.

CHAPTER TWO

The Actress and the Director

The Doctor: We have to touch it, you know. Otherwise it only gets worse.

Mrs. Vogeler screws up her eyes as if to shut the doctor out, then looks up again cautiously. The doctor is still there.

The Doctor: I do understand, you know. The hopeless dream of *being*. Not doing, just being. Aware and watchful every second. And at the same time the abyss between what you are for others and what you are for yourself. The feeling of dizziness and the continual burning need to be unmasked. At last to be seen through, reduced, perhaps extinguished. Every tone of voice a lie, an act of treason. Every gesture false. Every smile a grimace. The role of the wife, the role of the friend, the roles of mother and mistress, which is worst? Which has tortured you most? Playing the actress with the interesting face? Keeping all the pieces together with an iron hand and getting them to fit? Where did it break? Where did you fail? Was it the role of the mother that finally did it? It certainly wasn't your role as *Electra*. That gave you a rest. She actually got you to hold out a while more. She was an excuse for the more perfunctory performances you gave in your other roles, your 'real-life roles.' But when *Electra* was over, you had nothing left to hide behind, nothing to keep you going. No excuses. And so you were left with your demand for truth and your disgust. Kill yourself? No, too nasty, not to be done. But you could be immobile. You can keep quiet. Then at least you're not lying. You can cut yourself off, close yourself in. Then you don't have to play a part, put on a face, make false gestures. Or so you think. But reality plays tricks on you. Your hiding place isn't watertight enough. Life starts leaking in everywhere....

The Baltic island of Färo—the last piece of Swedish land before the Soviet Union begins—is a wind-swept, rocky, forsaken place, three hours from the Swedish mainland by car, plane, and ferry. Its only prominent inhabitant, besides flocks of sheep, is Ingmar Bergman. Sometimes when the ferry docks, clusters of tourists step off and rush to the high stone wall that circles Bergman's $100,000 home, hoping to boost themselves high enough to catch a glimpse of the famed director, a man of fifty-six, balding, of average height, his face set in an intense look of concentration, from a distance at least, entirely ordinary-looking. And when a film is in progress, they hope for sight of one of his family—cameraman Sven Nyquist, perhaps, or one of the actors and actresses who regularly appear in his films; Bibi Andersson or Ingrid Thulin or Max von Sydow or Liv Ullmann. During the five years that he and Liv lived together on the island, from 1966 to 1971, the tourists came to "Sheep Island" in flocks, particularly anxious to see the freckle-faced, golden-haired young woman whom the Swedish press had taken to calling Bergman's "little home companion," the woman who had supplanted his fourth wife and borne him a daughter out of wedlock.

Bergman came to Färo Island in 1965, and since then he has shot such films as *Persona*, *Shame*, *The Passion of Anna*, *The Hour of the Wolf*, *Cries and Whispers*, and parts of *Scenes from a Marriage* there. Bergman began making films in 1945, and *Scenes from a Marriage* was his thirty-fifth film. He has never made a film outside of Sweden, and he swears that he never will. Liv was the first non-Swedish actress he ever used, and Elliott Gould, who appeared in *The Touch*, is the only American who has appeared in a Bergman film. Like Federico Fellini, Michelangelo Antonioni and a few others, Bergman is one of the rare filmmakers whose films are highly personal statements. And of these, his output is the greatest, most varied and most personal.

He has achieved this status by controlling the production of his films to a degree that no other filmmaker has found to be either practical or possible. For a long time, until *Cries and Whispers* and *Scenes*, his films were considered to be uncommercial outside of Sweden. He was therefore not in a position to seek large amounts of money from financial sources, either studios in Hollywood or banks in Europe and the United States. But in any event, he did not seem to have the inclination to do this. His producer in Sweden, Svensk Filmindustri, was quite willing to back any project he submitted to them. Amazingly, Bergman's normal budget was $200,000 per film, and his shooting schedule six weeks. Until he made *Scenes*, which was financed by Swedish television, the only exception to this was *The Touch*, which Warners financed at Hollywood rates; $1,000,000 to Bergman and an extra $200,000 to pay Elliott Gould's salary. The only way Bergman would go along with the deal was for him to retain complete control of the film, including final cut, an arrangement that studios enter into with great reluctance, since studio executives normally feel that their final cut may well be a good deal more "commercial" than the filmmakers'.

In view of Bergman's reputation in 1972 as an art-house favorite, the deal was all the more surprising, and as it turned out, *The Touch* received highly mixed reviews, ranging from Penelope Gilliatt's in *The New Yorker*, which equated it with Bergman's other "masterpieces," *Persona* and *The Passion of Anna* (a minority view) to numerous others, among them, Andrew Sarris and John Simon, who felt that the movie was banal and Gould miscast in his role as a neurotic American who has a romance with Bibi Andersson.

Unlike many other filmmakers who become furious with what they feel is wrong-headed criticism and rush out to explain and defend themselves, Bergman does not react publicly to comments on his films. "The only judges of my work that is interesting to me," he has said, "is what a few friends think and what I think."

Film critic Pauline Kael said in 1965 that Bergman "made movies for people who don't like movies." What prompted this comment, the differing critical feelings about *The Touch*, and highly complicated and abstruse critical essays attempting to explain every Bergman film is precisely the fact that Bergman chooses to be a highly personal kind of filmmaker who writes his own scripts, chooses the actors to play in them (he writes to begin with having specific actors in mind), then directs them in their roles, having first mapped out all of the physical backgrounds and details of the film, and finally retires to a screening room to make the final cut.

Beyond that, Bergman is wonderfully skilled in the technical elements of moviemaking. He has worked with the same cameraman, Sven Nyquist, for fifteen years or so, and together, they have made Bergman's films marvelous examples of technical virtuosity. This same technical craftmanship, together with the highly personal content of Bergman's story ideas, have led critics into endless bouts of critical brow-knitting in an attempt to pin down exactly what Bergman means. Liv Ullmann believes all of this analyzing is the result of a natural critical impulse to complicate things. "There are no hidden meanings, no symbols. Those things are usually written in by the critics later. Ingmar wants to speak to the emotions. He writes out of his own torment and knowledge of people. If you know about people, you can follow his films."

But the questions remain, and Bergman's rare answers do not often help very much, though they do tend to confirm her feeling that it is all simply very personal to Bergman. For example, in *Cries and Whispers*, a film about three sisters living in a house, one of whom is dying of cancer, the walls of the house are red. Asked why this is so, Bergman explained: "Ever since my childhood, I have pictured the inside of the soul as a moist membrane in shades of red." Not having his explanation for numerous other special, strange, inexplicable Bergman touches in his films, his critics have come up with their own explanations, and of these there are as many as there are critics.

On the set, Bergman allows no outsiders—critics or fans—and to the actors and actresses in his company, whatever he wants them to do is almost always right. There are arguments over the actors' interpretation of a scene, or at times over some element or action in the script itself; but Bergman's acting company looks upon him with reverence as a very special kind of genius. There is the evidence of his films to begin with, of course. And from their experience with him, and the results on film, they have come to believe that part of this genius is his ability to bring out the best in them. Bergman is very sensitive to the wants of his company. "The actor," he says, "delivers his inner self at all times. If you feel scared or insecure, or feel there's something wrong with your nose, or with your saying this, or wrong with your gesture, you deliver nothing. But if the actor is in an atmosphere of security, he opens up like a flower."

Before a scene, Bergman will normally explain what the scene is all about but rarely talk about the actor's interpretation. As Liv says, he "feels you can *talk* a movie to pieces." When a scene is finished, he will offer a judgment. Liv explains: "He may say, 'Why not give it a little more?' or 'Try not giving so much.' But he never pushes. He chooses his actors for what they have to give and then he takes it from them. He makes you feel it is important to be an actor."

Bergman's way with actors is not just the result of working with the same ones over a period of years, as Liv Ullmann's performance in *Persona*, her first Bergman film, proves. It is rather a very special talent for communing with an actor's psyche. Elliott Gould felt it strongly when he was making *The Touch* with Bergman. Gould had doubts to start with about accepting the role. He came to Sweden and into the midst of Bergman's company as an outsider and a foreigner, but very shortly felt that Bergman was making marvelous use of his talents. "Bergman is sublime," Gould said in the middle of the shooting.

"When the take was over, I would get the chills. I would later feel very cold and know that I really allowed myself to be touched and that he took that extra thing that he felt was there. . . ."

Whatever Bergman's method for eliciting these responses from actors, there is no doubt of the brilliance of his results. The acting in his pictures almost invariably reveals the dimensions of characters with an extra-special clarity that few if any other directors achieve. As Penelope Gilliatt said of *The Touch*; "The film is full of acting moments that are physically miraculous, like brilliant fish drawn up on a line, like the memories of everyone."

Bergman seems to be able to work particularly well with women. He has, as John Simon has pointed out, built every film he has made around the shifting relationships between men and women. Even in a film such as *The Seventh Seal*, which chronicles the search of a knight for the meaning of life, the final resolution of the knight's discontent is accomplished through his return to his wife to find love and forgiveness. This concern with the man-woman relationship has become more and more simplified and clarified in Bergman's films since *Persona*, as he has stripped away much of his metaphysical probing to concentrate on the direct depiction of man and woman trying to solve their prickly and tricky combat with each other, the ultimate example being of course *Scenes from a Marriage*.

Bergman's own relationship with women has had a great bearing on his treatment of this theme in his films. Just as his male characters always need, in one way or another, a woman, Bergman himself has led a highly complicated existence in his relationships with women. Although he refuses completely to talk about his private life, he has admitted that he feels a special regard for working with women, because, he says, "they are more close to life" than men.

Bergman's success with Liv Ullmann has created a problem for her, since critics have been quick to say that only under Bergman's direction has she given truly brilliant performances. There is a good deal of truth to this, though Liv herself tends to discourage the idea. Certainly she has recognized Bergman's talent in directing women. "I think," she says, "he finds it easier to work with actresses because they are far less afraid of undressing—not their bodies but their minds. Men are always more reserved, both privately and professionally."

It may be that Bergman himself has only gradually become aware of how much he likes to have women "undress" before his camera. Certainly his earlier films, such as *The Seventh Seal* and *Winter Light*, were far less direct in their exploration of women than his later ones, beginning with *Persona*. Pointing this out, a number of critics have noted that the change began with his relationship to Liv Ullmann, and Bergman himself said in 1967 when *Persona* was being released in the United States that it marked the "beginning of a new phase." That turned out to be true. In *Shame*, *The Passion of Anna*, *Hour of the Wolf*, *Cries and Whispers*, and *Scenes from a Marriage*, Bergman made masterpieces about the problems of men and women in which he explored his own very personal concerns and knowledge, and in which he guided Liv Ullmann in a series of brilliant portraits on film.

Of all of these, *Persona* is perhaps the most original and most profound; a strange, jagged kind of film that has the same impact on a viewer as the best of Picasso's cubist distortions, a marvelously original film about masks and reality in which Liv Ullmann gave one of the screen's most expressive performances while uttering just two words—"No, don't"—in the course of a seventy-five-minute film.

* * *

"At first. I had to create an atmosphere of security, of calmness, of quietness, of stimulation, of love: yes, yes, of tenderness, you know. And then we are suddenly— we are all open...and I think when we rehearse we don't use our eyes so much as our ears, because the voices always tell you about the tensions inside, if something is wrong.

——Ingmar Bergman in a 1968 Public
Broadcast Laboratory interview

One day in 1964, Liv and Bibi Andersson, a friend of Liv's since they had made a film together, were walking down a street in Stockholm.

From the opposite direction, Ingmar Bergman approached.

"*Hey*," (Hello), Bibi said, smiling brightly.

"*Hey*," Bergman said, echoing the greeting, his dark eyes intent as always; and the two—the great director and a favored member of his acting "family"—engaged in conversation, catching up on events since they had last seen each other.

Then, suddenly, Bergman turned to Liv and said, "Would you like to be in one of my pictures?"

Liv blushed. She was still naturally shy at this time in her life, and she felt more so than usual in Bergman's presence, since she considered him to be "the best director in the world."

"Of course," she said, a smile lighting her face, thinking, "If a genius is like him, he isn't frightening." Yet, at the same time, as she has recalled, she felt "a little disappointed," because she thought Bergman was being insincere. "It was too much like a book," she says now, the unknown actress suddenly being offered a role by the renowned director, and I thought, 'How *glib* he is.'"

But Bergman was quite serious and, ultimately, his remark would lead to Liv Ullmann's role in *Persona* and completely change her life.

Bergman had seen Liv in a Danish-Norwegian film called *Short Is the Summer*. "I was a guest at Bibi Andersson's home," Bergman recalls, "and she and her husband showed me a film made in Norway. There was a Norwegian actress—Liv Ullmann—in the cast, and I looked at the two actresses and thought, "Those women are alike.""

That thought stayed filed in Bergman's mind. At the same time, he was impressed with Liv as an actress. When he met her, for the first time, on the street in Stockholm, he was working on a script in which he had written a small part for her. Then he fell ill with an ear infection (having the strange, almost Bergmanesque name of Morbus Ménièris) which severely affected his balance and when he was forced to go into the hospital for it, he stopped work on this script.

In the hospital, Bergman could look from his bed out a window to a chapel on the hospital grounds. "I knew that house [the chapel] was full of dead people," he says. "Of course, I felt it inside me somewhere that the whole atmosphere was one of death.... I was lying there, half dead, and suddenly I started to think of two faces, two intermingled faces, and that was the beginning, the place where it started."

"It" was the script of *Persona*, in which Bibi Andersson and Liv Ullmann play opposite each other, Liv as a famous actress who has decided never to speak again, and Bibi as the nurse who is assigned to take care of her, first in a hospital and then in a summer cottage on an island. *Persona* is an extremely complicated film, with many cross-currents of feeling, many elusive threads of narrative, action, and understanding. At the heart of it is the element of two personalities merging into each other, and this element is given eerie and consummate visual expression by Bergman when he projects half of Ullmann's face and half of Andersson's face to create a disturbing image of fusion on the screen; a face that is old and new, familiar and strange. So central is this filmic merging of faces to Bergman's conception that he has said of *Persona*, "It was possible only with these two actresses who look so much alike."

John Simon has called *Persona* Bergman's "most difficult film; indeed . . . probably the most difficult film ever made." He goes on to say that is "to film what *Ulysses* is to the novel: experiment raised to calm assurance . . . modernism becoming classicism before our eyes." Stanley Kauffmann feels it is an "exalted" film and analyzes it at great length in *Living Images*, concluding that it is Bergman's masterful attempt to present tragedy in totally modern terms. Most critics put it close to the top of the Bergman canon. In 1972 a poll showed that, difficult as it may be, *Persona* is regarded by critics around the world as one of their ten favorite films of all time.

The genesis of *Persona* in Bergman's mind, as described above, is of course only approximate. The reference points Bergman cites—noting how much alike Liv and Bibi looked, having the thought of two intermingled faces while lying in a hospital bed—may represent only the tip of an iceberg of inspiration for the idea of the film in Bergman's conscious and unconscious mind. But his account is typical of the way that Bergman describes his process of creation. As he analyzes this process, the starting point is one tiny moment of the whole: "It always starts very secretly," he said in an interview with John Simon. "It starts with a sort of tension or a specific scene, some lines, a picture or something, a piece of music."

In any event, starting from his image of intermingled faces in the hospital, Bergman wrote the script for *Persona*, having Liv and Bibi in mind for the roles, and then, when he had been released from the hospital and was back at work, he told them of the project.

Liv Ullmann & Ingmar Bergman

Hearing the news, Liv felt "very honored." Bergman had never used a non-Swedish actress before.

Like all of Bergman's films, *Persona* was shot in an amazingly short time—just six weeks in the spring of 1966—and this includes time spent reshooting interior scenes first done at the studio in Stockholm on location on Fåro Island. When Liv came to Sweden to work on the film, she was just twenty-five, an actress who had achieved considerable success in Norway on stage and in films, but one who was basically unknown to the larger film world, much less to the rest of Scandinavia. Bergman was forty-six, and if not universally acknowledged to be what Liv considered him to be, the greatest director in the world, certainly considered one of contemporary cinema's most outstanding filmmakers.

It was not surprising, considering her shyness and relative obscurity as an actress and his towering reputation, that Liv was totally in awe of him. If this made the situation difficult to begin with, the nature of her role made it even more so, for she was charged with creating a highly complex and multidimensional character without having the possibility of speaking lines. "At first," Liv says now, "I was scared to death. I blushed whenever Bergman said a word." Liv was living in Stockholm with Bibi Andersson and Bibi's husband. "If I had not had Bibi there," Liv says, "I wouldn't have gotten through." Bibi, too, Liv recalls, was quite nervous and even "broke out in spots." But Bergman's instinct in choosing Liv was, as it turned out, right on target as usual, though he may have had a second thought or two at the start, since Liv has said that she and Bibi both heard later that "there was a lot of talk during the first week about canceling the whole project."

Bergman has never confirmed this. He has said, "From the beginning, when I worked with Liv I was always impressed by her passion of expressing herself—with her face, her body, her voice. Liv, like the best of all creative artists, has marvelous integrity and enormous faith in her own ability."

That judgment coincides with Liv's remembrance of how she responded on the set of *Persona*. "Slowly," she says, "I understood that he was kind and nice, and then "I started to trust myself." As she created the character of actress Alma Vogeler, she relied almost completely on her innermost feelings. She found the part very difficult and not one that she could particularly relate to out of her own experiences. She did not see herself as "an actress at the height of her career," as Alma Vogeler was supposed to be, although her own career in Norway might easily have allowed her to do so, since she had scored an outstanding success in 1960 in her first role, that of Anne in *The Diary of Anne Frank* when she was just seventeen, and since then had appeared on stage and in film in a great variety of roles, always to critical acclaim. On the other hand, she could hardly relate strongly to Alma's disturbed nature. She had been married at twenty to a Norwegian doctor, and though this marriage was shaky at the moment, she was far from being anguished enough to withdraw mutely from the world.

Thinking about her role as Alma, she felt that Alma's experiences were for the most part not her own—though, interestingly enough, she concluded that Alma represented, in part at least, Bergman. "I felt very strongly when I was doing the movie," she said later, "that I was actually *being* Ingmar." The parallel was not at all farfetched—Bergman lying in a hospital bed reflecting on death had written a script about a great actress who withdraws mutely from the world. Still, Liv felt that if Bergman tried to verbalize his conceptions of how she should play the role, tried to verbalize the inner mechanisms of Alma's personality, she wouldn't truly be able to understand. As a talented actress does, she relied instead of verbalization on what she sensed about the character, and, as she says now, she was able to sense even more about Alma than she realized at the time. This was a confirmation of Bergman's feelings about her intuition. "I got to do what I felt," she says, "and Bergman never questioned me."

Bergman discusses his feelings about intuition: "My whole life I have trained my intuition. It's a sort of track I travel on the whole time"—undoubtedly the heart of his directorial technique in handling actors. As Liv describes it, "Ingmar does not talk too much about how to play a scene. He gives blocking. When he sees nothing coming from an actor, then he draws on what he knows about an actor's private life or he gives a little clue to the scene." As he watched Liv on the set of *Persona*, he was eminently satisfied and offered a minimum of guidance. And as Liv saw the shooting move forward with no great problems, as she felt her interpretation to be right and effective, her confidence rose. "I didn't speak to him very much in the beginning," she says, "because I was very shy. But I had a great feeling for him." The Bergman magic worked once again, and the actor's response to it drew from her a performance of wonderful range and emotion. The fact that it was a performance she was basically arranging herself instead of being "babied" into made it all the more confidence-building to her.

Bergman's method of handling actors, his *laissez faire* attitude, is noteworthy in itself and also because he is an extremely complex and demanding man. He has, at various times, described himself as "neurotic" (but not about his work), as "hysterical," and as a "relatively inhibited, shy, timid person who has trouble establishing deeper relationships." He is also, needless to say, enormously intelligent, almost compulsively creative, and the amalgam of all these qualities (and others) is well reflected in the kind of films he makes.

That the demanding and rigorous quality of his nature does not overwhelm his sympathy for and sensitivity to actors and their requirements for creating a role is all the more surprising because his description of himself as "timid" is, in the context of his film making, quite misleading. As writer-director-producer, he is totally aware of his needs and goals and, in fact, he can be highly temperamental, difficult, and demanding on the set.

Bergman himself recognizes his steely perfectionism in the realm of filmmaking. He has called himself a "pedant" and noted that he is, despite his timidity and shyness, "very aggressive." Max von Sydow echoes this judgment by describing Bergman as "a man very anxious to stay in command." Yet, for the most part, he keeps his aggressiveness under tight control in working with actors. By doing so, by encouraging his acting family to follow their own instincts in creating a role, he has elicited masterful performances from them in film after film. And beyond that, he has achieved a further benefit in making the actors proud of their own self-reliance and independent powers of creation, so that they are happy to work for him over and over again, instead of for another director who might offer them more money but keep a much tighter rein on their creativity.

On the set of *Persona*, once Liv had adjusted to the newness of the experience, there was a happy atmosphere. "We had a wonderful time," Liv says, "always joking. We just thought we were making this small film on an island and nobody would ever see it, and then it became a classic...."

There was another reason for the happiness on the set of *Persona* besides the way the picture was progressing. Not too long after she had met Ingmar Bergman, Liv knew that she was in love with him, and that he loved her in return. When the shooting was finished, instead of returning to Norway and her husband, she stayed on Färo with him.

CHAPTER THREE

Becoming Alive

When you get to know him or catch him off-guard, he's terribly vulnerable. He touches some kind of mother in me. He did so even then, [in 1967] despite our differences in age.

> —Liv Ullmann in a 1974 interview.

Love. Goethe said of it: "When faced with the overwhelming evidence of another's superiority, there is nothing for the ego to do but declare its love." It is, of course, the lovers' apprehension of just what that superiority consists of that makes love a story with an infinite number of beginnings, middles, and ends.

As all lovers do, Liv and Bergman took into their affair their mysterious past, the years of their lives before they had met. Not knowing the true outlines of their separate existences, there was no way for them to know precisely how the soil and seed of their past and personalities had made their present flower. They could only enjoy the sunshine.

For Liv, life before she met Bergman had been an almost devious amalgamation of ups and downs, a curious compound of win and lose. When she was six years old, her father died as the result of an eerie, bizarre accident. As World War II approached, the family had been living in Tokyo, where her father, Viggo Ullmann, worked as a civil engineer, and where Liv was born in 1938. But with the German conquest of Norway in 1940, and with the clear evidence of Japan's commitment to Hitler's dreams of conquest, Viggo Ullmann took his family to Canada, where so many Norwegian exiles had gathered outside of Toronto that the outpost was known as "Little Norway." Here Liv and her sister, Janna, played with the children of the Norwegian royal family, Prince Harald and Princesses Ragnhild and Astrid while their father served in the Norwegian Royal Air Force.

One day in 1943, Liv's father suffered the nightmare accident that would ultimately take his life. On duty at the airfield, he walked into the whirring propeller of a plane. His injuries brought him within a hairsbreadth of death but miraculously he seemed to recover and slowly the family gave rein to the hope that he would survive. They came to New York so that he could be treated in that city's excellent hospitals. But the hope turned out to be illusory, and in 1944 Viggo Ullmann died. When the war ended, Liv's mother, also named Janna, took Liv and her nine-year-old sister back to

Norway. They settled in Trondheim, a city of some 80,000 inhabitants 250 miles north of Oslo.

If there is a particular Scandinavian landscape and a particular Scandinavian character, one might perhaps find it in pure form in a city like Trondheim, whose geographical location gives life there a special quality. Trondheim is just 125 miles south of the Arctic Circle, and its inhabitants are subjected to an almost schizophrenic alternation of light and dark. In the summer, when the days are long, darkness lasts for just a short time—at the height of the season, from 11 P.M. to 3 A.M. At the height of winter, the opposite extreme applies, and daylight lasts only from 8 A.M. to 4 P.M.

These extremes of light and dark have their effect. The long, shadowed winter can induce severe depression; the gleaming light of summer in turn elicits a great surge of energy, an almost manic euphoria. This schizophrenic environment has its general parallel, in fact, in what has to be called, for want of a more precise term, the Scandinavian personality, which tends, as many observers have noted, to swing between the heights of a charming, feckless love of fun and pleasure and an equally intense tendency to gloom and depression, with, somewhere in the middle, a devotion to duty, to hard work, a fear of God, and a concern for the fate of one's soul.

To some observers, these swings of elation and despair are less pronounced in the Norwegians than in the Swedish. It is generally true that Norway is more "backward" than Sweden, perhaps a generation behind in its commitment to those trends we think of as specifically "modern," the "welfare state," industrialization, and sexual freedom. Sweden throughout its history has moved a step further into the footlights than Norway, has always had a few more lines to speak in the play of European nations than its neighbor to the west. Norwegians tend to be more reserved and self-contained, more committed to the process of living without questioning too much why that process applies to them. The suicide rate in Sweden has always been substantially higher than that in Norway. And yet, that great questioner of modern dogmas, Henrik Ibsen, was a Norwegian.

In Trondheim, Liv's mother ran a bookshop. She never remarried and never regretted not having done so. Her devotion to her dead husband was strong and unwavering, a feeling she communicated to her daughters, who, quite naturally, felt the lack of a father.

The war years had been a dislocation that it would not have been too difficult for a young girl to forget in the security of a tranquil life in her native country. Liv's memory of Canada and New York was quite hazy. "It's strange," she says now, "my mother has never told me about that period, and my memory is so very poor that I don't remember anything about New York except the Statue of Liberty." But, living in a fatherless home, the dislocation continued. She felt the absence of her father all the more keenly because her mother, in her bereavement and devotion, conveyed to her and her sister the idea of a fantasy father; one who would always protect her and take care of her if she were ever in any distress.

Of her dead father, Liv has said, "I don't remember him. It is very sad. I remember somebody carrying me upstairs and putting me in a bed, and it was very safe. That's all. Which is not much."

Much more to her at the time was the possibility of writing to the seemingly real father her mother often spoke of, and she composed long letters "to my father in heaven, telling him all my thoughts, or pleading with him to come back." This was no casual thing. If she saw a Norwegian airman on the street, she would run after him, breathless in the desire that it be the moment when she would get her father back.

She was, in truth, a superimaginative little girl, and her bubbling mind could misinterpret her own presence as well as her father's absence. She felt, without any justification except the thought itself, overwhelmingly awkward and inadequate about herself. She was indeed extremely shy, but beyond that, she was convinced that she was unattractive and she was bedeviled at the humiliation of being flat-chested. She also thought that she had ugly toes, and she used to keep her shoes on at the beach in order to obscure them.

The feeling that this catalog of sins produced in her, the feeling that there was no hope for her, led to a predictable result. Her contemporaries took her at her own estimation, and she literally had no friends at all, male or female. At dancing school, the boys never asked her to dance. So intense was her longing to change this isolation that once, when a girl sat down next to her in the school cafeteria and spoke to her for a little while, Liv returned to the same spot day after day, hoping the girl would appear again. She never did, and Liv concluded that she was "nothing." She would never make it.

At the same time that she experienced these shattering rejections, Liv was being brought up in a highly conventional middle-class way. Her mother was protective of her, and Liv was led to believe that "nothing was expected of me. I was brought up to be very old-fashioned, to be well behaved, and I thought if I was that way I wouldn't harm anybody and I wouldn't be found out."

Liv's only true friend was her grandmother. "She

lived in a world of unreality," Liv says. "We took long walks in the woods, and she made me conscious of nature. Sometimes we went to the cinema three times a day."

To the fantasy of films, Liv added a passion for books. She really didn't care too much for school, feeling that "there was no life in learning history places and dates." But after school she would retreat to her mother's bookstore and "sit in a corner and read."

And at the core of her secret world, which was perhaps more real than the real one, was the desire to be an actress, "to show them" that she was, in actuality, not the shy, awkward girl everyone thought her to be, but a creature of mood and power, capable of stirring those around her (but an audience she didn't have to meet face to face) to extremes of emotion, and in so doing, to prove that she was "alive." She wrote many plays, a number of them religious ones "all about people hoping for miracles."

At school she formed a dramatic group in which she became the leading writer and the leading actress as well. "Life to me was onstage," she says now of her feeling then. "I don't believe you choose the theater because you're shy," she explains. "I chose the theater because that was my way of expressing myself."

When she was seventeen, she told her mother of her acting ambitions and suggested that it would be a good idea if she set out to realize them by going to study in England. Her mother's response was far from enthusiastic. Only after a family friend suggested that this response might be selfishness rather than motherly wisdom did she agree, and off Liv went to a boarding school in England.

There is perhaps no institution in the world which at first taste is as stuffy and strange as an English boarding school. The girls all wore uniforms and the very first night at dinner the headmistress told Liv:

"We don't put our elbows on the table while dining." It was little wonder that the seventeen-year-old from Trondheim, Norway, speaking English with some trace of an accent, shy and unsure, tall and a bit gawky in her movements, her red-gold hair framing a somewhat chubby face covered with freckles, should have felt out of place. No doubt many of the English girls felt the same—but had no possibility of calling a mother, as Liv did after two weeks, and announcing: "I can't stay here."

With her mother's permission, Liv left the school, which was about two hours' from London, and went to live at a London YWCA while she studied acting at a drama school. That was much more to Liv's liking. She had a teacher she thought was "marvelous" and she felt she was learning a good deal about acting. At the same time, she was, for the first time in her life, pretty much on her own. She was freer somehow to make friends than she had been in Trondheim. London was like starting a new life, and none of her new companions were aware of the details of her old one back in Norway. She was free not to be as awkward and as shy as she had been. And besides there was a whole new and wonderful city to see and learn about.

When she returned to Norway eight months later, she was ready to take the examination for the state theater school in Oslo. Liv was full of hope. There was one problem: those in charge of the school watched her audition and then gave their considered judgment. She was refused entrance on the school's most solid ground; that she had no talent.

Amazingly undaunted, she looked around for alternatives and found a place in the repertory theater in the city of Stavanger, 75 miles south of Oslo and about the same size as Trondheim. The company was about to put on *The Diary of Anne Frank*, the story of a fifteen-year-old Jewish girl in Amsterdam whose family had hidden in an attic to escape the Nazis during the war, only, finally, to be discovered and taken away to a concentration camp. The play had been adapted from the best-selling book by two American authors, Albert Hackett and Frances Goodrich, and had achieved success first on Broadway and then throughout Europe, even and particularly in Germany.

In 1957, twelve years after the war had ended, the story of the Nazi terror was still capable of opening old emotional wounds in Europe. Norway had fought the invaders as best it could after the occupation, and Norway's resistance fighters were among Europe's bravest. For Liv, the war had been somewhat far away, but her grandfather, her father's father, had fought in the resistance, been captured by the Germans and taken away to Auschwitz, never to be heard of again. (Seven years later, traveling in Poland with her friend, Bibi Andersson, Liv met a man who had shared a bed with Halvdan Ullmann, and who was able to tell her all of the details of his last days.)

The best role in the play was of course Anne, the bright, lively, imaginative and sensitive teen-ager around whose problems of growing up the play revolves. Liv was chosen for the part. The identification and the resonances were there, and so was the talent to convert her feelings into theatrical energy. She opened to rave reviews, and suddenly the dream was a reality. She was an actress and, finally, "alive." Looking back at her triumph in 1972, Liv said: "It was a lovely part. You couldn't miss. The theater really belonged to you. I was truly lucky. It will never be that way again."

It was of course more than the "lovely part" that gave her a triumph, and to have her talent confirmed at last, and in such a wonderful flash of success, was storybook stuff, and a great dose of vitamins for her sometimes anemic ego. And despite her feeling that it will never happen again, it has become obvious that, whether Liv demurs out of modesty or still has real doubts, it will be that way for her over and over again, if "that way" refers to an actress making a character come breathtakingly alive on stage or in a film.

Other roles followed and Liv's stature and reputation grew. She spent three years in Stavanger, then went to Oslo as part of the company at Det Norske Teatret and later to the Norwegian National Theater. For whatever reasons, she was almost always cast in roles that called for her to be "a good and sweet" woman, including Ophelia, Gretchen in Goethe's *Faust* and Saint Joan in Shaw's play, though this role calls for a good deal of steel as well.

Far more at ease with herself after her success at Stavanger, she could feel too that the awkwardness of her adolescence was fading away like a distant memory—and yet, the memory of it remained. And she could see as well that, far from her young image of herself as unattractive, she was physically becoming a quite different person. Her body filled out (she no longer had to pad her bust, as she used to do in London) and her face had firmed, the fleshy softness of her teen-age years falling away. With her deep-blue, cornflower eyes and her striking mane of golden hair, she was indeed a beautiful woman.

All of these circumstances gave her a much greater feeling of self-possession. There were many friends now, and beaus, too. One was a doctor from Oslo named Jacob Stang, and when he proposed, she accepted. She was twenty when they married; he was twenty-five; an ideal difference in the common view. "I had a strong idea of a man," she says now. "He was everything I thought my father was, everything my mother told me about him: always safe, nice and understanding. As it turned out, my first husband had as many false expectations of me as I had of him."

Ingmar Bergman and Liv Ullmann.

Liv Ullmann and Max von Sydow during the production of SHAME at Fårö 1967.

Bibi Anderson and Liv Ullmann in PERSONA (1966). The film which started Bergman's cooperation with Liv Ullmann. Photo *Svensk Film.*

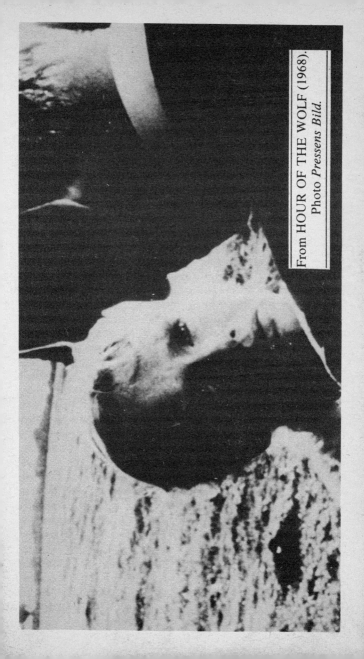

From HOUR OF THE WOLF (1968).
Photo *Pressens Bild.*

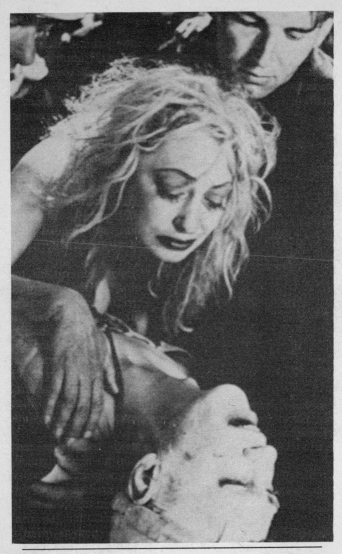

Gudrun Brost (Alma) and Anders Ek (Frost in Bergman's first "classic" THE NAKED NIGHT (1953).
Photo *Sandrews*.

Ingmar Bergman together with his photographer Sven Nykvist, who received Oscar prize for his Bergman photo.

Liv Ullmann as Kristina in THE EMIGRANTS
(1971) with her daughter Linn.
Photo *Pressens Bild.*

Liv Ullmann as Kristina in THE EMIGRANTS (1971) with Max von Sydow. Photo *Pressens Bild.*

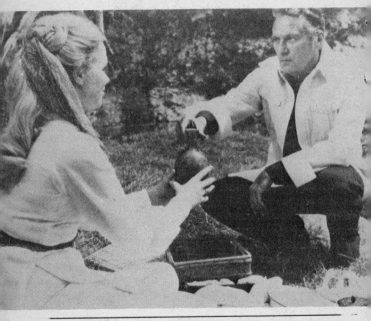

Liv Ullmann in Hollywood. With Peter Finch in LOST HORIZON. Photo *Pressens Bild.*

CHAPTER FOUR

Bergman

*He was a very young man then, tall, thin, with black
hair and burning black eyes. . . . Here, I thought, was a
refreshing young talent, a little crazy, perhaps,
certainly immature, but with a lot of bold and fanciful
ideas.*

> ——Carl Anders Dymling, for many years
> Bergman's producer as the president of
> Svensk Filmindustri

Three scenes from Ingmar Bergman's childhood.
One. He is in his nursery. He has a magic lantern, a
small metal box with a carbide lamp ("I can still

remember the smell of the hot metal") with which he can project slide pictures on the flowered nursery wallpaper. He flashes Little Red Riding Hood on the wall, a familiar story. There is the wolf, with his tail and his "gaping red mouth." To the small boy, he is not the wolf at all, he is the devil, "strangely real yet incomprehensible," an "emissary of evil and persecution."

Two. He is five years old, sitting under the table in his grandmother's dining room, recovering from the measles. It is a day between winter and spring. Sunbeams slant through the high windows of the room. Cathedral bells toll outside. In the next apartment, a piano is being played, "waltzes, nothing but waltzes." To the boy, the moving rays of the sun make a special sound that he can "listen" to. The sun moves across a large picture of Venice hanging on the wall and in the picture the water begins to flow, the pigeons in St. Mark's Square flutter up, people talk and gesture to each other. Now the piano music and the sound of the bells come not from outside the room but from the picture itself.

Three. He is even younger than five, lying in bed in his nursery, staring at a window blind. The blind is an ordinary black one. It is either dusk or dawn, when "everything becomes living and a bit frightening," when the world is no longer the ordinary one he knows when his mother is present, but a strange, "silent solitude." Forms appear on the surface of the blind: "They were neither little men nor animals, nor heads, nor faces, but *things for which no name exists!*" The forms free themselves from the blind and move across the room. To the boy, they are "pitiless, impassive, and terrifying." They disapear only when it becomes completely dark or light, or when he falls asleep.

Ingmar Bergman recalls these memories lovingly, linking them to his adult life as a filmmaker.

"Filmmaking," he says, "is... plunging with one's deepest roots back into the world of childhood." Bergman remembers also that he received his first film projector when he was nine years old. On this machine, "mystifying and fascinating," he projected his first piece of film, about nine feet in length, which showed a young girl asleep on the prairie, waking, stretching, standing up and walking with arms outstretched out of the picture. This film he played until it wore out.

"I have often wondered," he says now, "what could have fascinated me so much [about the film and projector] and what, even today, still fascinates me in exactly the same way."

Perhaps, one clue lies in a particular aspect of Ingmar Bergman's personality. Trying to account for his "artistic activity," Bergman has explained that from early childhood, he felt "a need to show what I had achieved; progress in drawing, the ability to bounce a ball against the wall, my first strokes in the water." But try as he might, he never got as much attention as he wanted. "And so, when reality no longer sufficed, I began to make things up, regaling my contemporaries with tremendous stories of my secret exploits." And when skepticism began to greet these exaggerations, he "withdrew from fellowship and kept my dreams to myself. A contact-seeking child, beset by fantasies, I was quickly transformed into a hurt, cunning, and suspicious daydreamer."

Are Bergman's films the transformation of his daydreams into objects of attention, a transformation made possible by the magic of the motion picture camera? No doubt. But of course they are much else as well. As Bergman says, "a daydreamer is not an artist except in his dreams."

The dining room table Ingmar Bergman sat under,

the nursery he slept in, were in the university city of Uppsala, 50 miles north of Stockholm, where Ernest Ingmar Bergman was born on July 14, 1918, the son of a Lutheran minister. When Ingmar was six years old, his father was appointed court chaplain to the royal family in Stockholm, and it was in this cosmopolitan city that Bergman grew up.

As Bergman has said, "A child who is born and brought up in a vicarage acquires an early familiarity with life and death behind the scenes. Father performed funerals, marriages, baptisms, gave advice, and prepared sermons. The devil was an early acquaintance, and in the child's mind there was a need to personify him." Hence the wolf in Red Riding Hood, which was soon replaced by the devil in its true form as he absorbed the theology of the Luthern church. A minister's son, after all, may turn out to be an atheist, but not before he's heard all of the arguments.

In 1960, before he had begun to explore from a specifically religious stance the questions of faith and doubt that are central to such films as *The Seventh Seal*, *Through a Glass Darkly*, and *Winter Light*, Bergman commented on the role of religion in his life and in his films. "To me," he said, "religious problems are continuously alive. I never cease to concern myself with them...." Yet, he went on, religion on an emotional level, "religious sentimentality," was "something I got rid of long ago—I hope." His concern was an intellectual one: "the relationship of my mind to my intuition."

Along with his religious feeling, Bergman absorbed from what he described as "his strict middle-class home" an atmosphere of "hearty wholesomeness"—useful, he thought later, because it gave him something to scorn and rebel against, a "wall to sharpen himself against." For this he was grateful, and he was grateful, too, for being taught efficiency, punctuality, and a sense of financial responsibility—bourgeois values he considers important to the artist because they help him to set strict standards for himself.

Yet, outside the Bergman home as Bergman grew to manhood in the Sweden of the 1930s, many of the old values were breaking down, the power of the Protestant church declining, the power of the welfare state increasing, to the detriment, as many saw it, of "bourgeois" virtues such as thrift, responsibility, and ambition. And for the rest of Europe, war loomed as Nazi Germany began to fulfill the evil destiny Hitler mapped for it. The fact that Sweden would not align itself in this struggle but remain neutral instead induced guilt, shame, and anger in many Swedes who raged against this moral flabbiness.

When he was sixteen, in 1935, Bergman, describing himself as a "political virgin," went to Germany as an exchange student staying at the home of a German minister, one of whose four sons, Bergman's age, was a member of the *Hitlerjugend*. Bergman saw German children in school reading *Mein Kampf* (in religion class), attended the tenth-anniversary Nazi party celebration in Weimar and was "fascinated" by it all. It was not until after the war began, Bergman has recalled, that "we realized in Sweden what had happened in Germany." Bergman found this realization "terribly painful" and in the first of his film scripts ever produced, *Torment*, he exorcised some of that pain. Much later, having reflected on what can happen to "ordinary people in such a war," he translated his concerns and conclusions into *Shame*.

When war broke out in 1940, Bergman was in his third year at Stockholm University, studying art and history, but already thinking of story ideas and taking part in student theatrical activities. Having completed his military service, in 1941 Bergman took a job as an assistant director of the Royal Opera, while continuing to direct student and amateur theatrical productions, which were put on with limited budgets in small theaters.

In 1942, Carl Anders Dymling, the newly appointed president of Svensk Filmindustri, saw one of Bergman's productions, thought him "a refreshing young talent," and hired him to rewrite scripts at the studio in Räsunda, outside of Stockholm. While working on projects given him by the studio, he also wrote a script of his own—actually a short novel rather than a scenario, a form he followed for years afterward in presenting new ideas for films. This was *Torment*, and it made a strong impression on Dymling, who described it as "a startling experience" and Bergman as "an angry young man—long before they became the fashion."

Torment was produced in 1944 by Svensk Filmindustri, directed by Alf Sjöberg, the most towering figure in Swedish film history, with Ingmar Bergman as the assistant director. The visual style of the film was clearly Sjöberg's, and he made a number of suggestions for the final shooting script. But the script remained Bergman's, and a look at it tells a good deal about Bergman's state of mind at the time, his powers of creation and the paths he would follow in later films.

In the main narrative line, a young man named Lars-Eric, still in school and living at home, meets a beautiful prostitute named Bertha and befriends her. For him, she represents an escape and a revolt from the oppressive aspects of his life at home and in school. He is, essentially, a young man in revolt against what he sees as the repressiveness suffocating tyrannies of school life, the passivity of the majority of the students, the narrowness of family life, the complacency and injustice of society in general. The purest manifestation of evil that Lars-Eric faces is the teacher Caligula (the name seems blatantly obvious), a capriciously cruel man who tyrannizes the students and attempts to make love to Bertha.

Lars-Eric is the outsider, the romantic nonconformist. It is through his eyes that the story is told. It is his experiences and his reactions to them that establish the stance from which the film records its criticism of people and institutions. There is more than a suggestion in the film that this criticism can be extended to Sweden's failure to take a stand against Nazi Germany, since, in many ways, Caligula can be seen as a Hitler.

The film was a solid success in Sweden and internationally, though American audiences saw only a mutilated version. It was praised for its psychological truth and its realism (heightened and distorted, to be sure), qualities not always present in Swedish films. For Swedish audiences, part of its appeal was that it dramatized a conflict that was in the air, the conflict between the old authoritarian upbringing of children and the new freedom that was developing in Sweden.

The autobiographical base of the film was evident in its observation of school and home and in its dramatization of a crisis point in the life of a young man of high intelligence and artistic ambitions anxious to "attract the attention of grown-ups." In outline, the story of *Torment* might seem decidedly shopworn. In one sense, the story comes down to boy meets girl, boy loses girl, boy is a better person for it, and if the girl is a prostitute rather than a virginal young creature, that, too, is hardly a fresh approach. Characteristic of the genre also was the resolution. Lars-Eric's "torment" makes him stronger, better able to face the adult world and make his way on his own terms. What adolescent, artistic or not, has not felt, at one time or another, life to be out of step with his feelings and emotions?

Yet Bergman was able to take these clichés and

breathe life into them, a characteristic of his later work as well. It is Bergman's talent and intelligence that makes *Torment* individual and compelling as a film, Bergman's personal statement of youthful rebellion and the conflict between generations, coupled with acute observations of the people and society of his time, that lifts it out of the ordinary.

If *Torment* had neither the scope nor the power of *Young Werther* or *Tonio Kroger*, it was nevertheless in their tradition, revealing Bergman, like Goethe and Mann, to be a writer capable of standing off from himself to take the "raw material" of his life and fashion it into a work of art. Beyond that, the film uncovered the topography of Bergman's film landscape. It was "serious," not an entertainment. It wrestled with questions of conduct and morality, good and evil, right and wrong. It presented man trying to control his destiny, making choices, contending with forces within and without himself. These conflicts and questions, with others added, would continue to occupy him.

Torment inaugurated the first phase of Bergman's film career. The next year, 1945, he directed his first film, *Crisis*, which had a script adapted by him from a Swedish play entitled *Moderdyret*. In the next ten years, with Svensk Filmindustri as producer in almost every case, he directed fifteen more films. Of these, he wrote the screenplay for twelve (three of these were co-authored); in eight of them starting with his own original idea. In addition, he wrote another original screenplay and provided Svensk Filmindustri with two story ideas that were produced as films.

Bergman's film output was all the more prodigious because he was heavily involved in the theater at the same time. In 1944 he became head of the Halsingborg Municipal Theater; in 1946 producer at the Gothenburg Municipal Theater. From 1952 until 1959 he was the director of the Civic Theater in Malmö, and in 1960 he was appointed a director of Sweden's leading theater, the Royal Dramatic Theater in Stockholm, becoming its managing director in 1967. Between 1938 and 1962, Bergman staged something like seventy productions, as well as thirty radio performances and five plays for television, achievements which confirm his intense capacity for work.

In his stage career, Bergman achieved a high reputation more quickly than in films, and several of the plays he presented in Sweden went to Paris, London, and other European cities. Among these was *Hedda Gabler*, which he directed in London in a production starring Maggie Smith that William Wolf of *Cue* magazine described as "a stunning accomplishment." Bergman's work in the theater has been more conservative, or at least more conventional, than his film work; yet there is a strong connection between the two media for him. In the theater, as in films, one of his great strengths has been his ability to work with actors, to get from them powerful performances that are yet exactly right for the play, and to submerge these performances into a concept of the play as a whole; to create a unified ensemble that brings a play to life on stage. In fact, it is safe to say that it was Bergman's stage work that provided him with the opportunity to perfect this talent. In the theater as well, he found a supply of acting talent that he could use in his films. Among others, Bibi Andersson, Ingrid Thulin, Harriet Andersson and Max von Sydow all worked with him in the theater and in his films, too.

Like most artists, Bergman had to shape and hone his talents, and this was more true in the case of films than with his theater work, mainly because in films he was moving very much in his own personal direction. Beyond that, he came to filmmaking with great desire but no practical experience, and the making of films is an art further away from one's normal life experiences than directing a stage play. Bergman's growth as a filmmaker is clearly evident in looking at his early films. He himself has pronounced his second film, the first one he directed, a film called *Crisis*, "an unsuccessful movie," and has paid tribute to Loren Marmstedt, who was his producer for his next film, *It Rains on Our love*, released in 1946, for teaching him filmmaking "from scratch."

Like most artists, too, Bergman had strong ideas about his work, and the conflict between pleasing himself—even as an outright beginner—which is to say, perfecting his talent on his own terms, and adjusting to the outside realities and pressures of the film business (which has more of these than almost any other business one can name) was not easily resolved.

Some insight into this problem comes from Carl Anders Dymling, who set down a description in retrospect of Bergman as a young filmmaker. He was, Dymling recalled, "a rebel-child. "He has always been a problem," Dymling went on, "not only to others but also to himself, and I think he will remain so. He is a high-strung personality, passionately alive, enormously sensitive, very short-tempered, sometimes quite ruthless in the pursuit of his own goals, suspicious, stubborn, capricious, most unpredictable. His will-power is extraordinary." In other words, he was a real handful if you were on the other side of the fence in the question of transferring an artistic vision from its conceiver's mind to the screen—*at a profit*.

Fighting for his own ideas and ideals, Bergman, in the period from 1944 to 1956, established himself only slowly and not without enormous criticism, as an international filmmaker of stature. The first of his films that achieved general international recognition was *Summerplay* (1951), called *Illicit Interlude* in America, which had a script co-authored with

Bergman by Herbert Gravenius, another Bergman has named as a strong influence on his filmmaking, from a manuscript by Bergman. It tells the story of a ballerina of twenty-eight, in despair with ler life, who looks back on her first love when she was fifteen, a love which ended when the young student she was to marry accidentally killed himself diving off a cliff. At the film's end, she has come to terms with her loss, is ready to accept new love and to devote herself with hope and dedication to her career as a ballerina. The seriousness of the film is lightened by scenes of great tenderness and joy as the young couple exult in their summer of happiness. Bergman regards this film as his first "mature" one. Pauline Kael called it a "breakthrough" for him and noted that Bergman had "found his style" in it.

In contrast, *The Naked Night*, produced in 1953, is unrelievedly bleak and somber—except for an ending thrust of hope that is only one pine in its forest of despair. Brilliantly executed, it uses the story of a traveling circus to explore, in the most powerful way Bergman had yet been able to achieve, some of his major themes: love and the humiliation it can produce; the artist's uncertain life versus the bourgeois comfort and respectability of the nonartist; the difficulties of true feeling and communication between man and woman.

The Naked Night brought to perfection for the first time all of the element's in Bergman's filmmaking repertoire. He opened with a flashback, shot overexposed to give it a visual quality quite different from the rest of the film (Pauline Kael erroneously concluded that it was shot on different film stock; other critics labeled it a dream). It used highly effective natural sounds instead of music to underline and heighten the action. The brilliant screenplay by Bergman presents a highly complex experience, in which many themes and subthemes are explored, with wonderful economy and in highly effective dramatic terms. There is no didacticism in Bergman's script; the themes emerge naturally from the action. The interpretation of these themes, what the picture actually means, is very much a matter of the viewer's judgment as it is, one could say, in most works of art. Bergman got performances that were perfect in every detail from his cast, which included Harriett Andersson, Ake Grönberg and Anders Ek in major roles. So brilliantly did he cast the film that the illusion emerged of a Bergman repertory company whose members had been playing together for years.

The richness and complexity of *Naked Night* led to varied critical responses which, in the main, were on the plus side, though Pauline Kael called it "powerfully awful," unrelievedly despairing. She also felt that it was Bergman's replay of German expressionism of the twenties, a response that seems off-the-mark considering its technical advances, the freshness of Bergman's visualization, the tightness of his direction and editing, all of which make the highly controlled quality of his sometimes heightened realism a far cry from the sentimental excesses of expressionism.

Unlike many films greeted with enthusiasm and later seen to be of far inferior stature, *The Naked Night* has retained its power over the years, and is now regarded as one of the cinema's great films, Bergman's first masterpiece.

CHAPTER FIVE

The Actress and the Director

It doesn't fit; nothing hangs together when you start to think. And all that bad conscience for things that don't matter. You understand what I mean? Can you be quite different people, all next to each other, at the same time? And then what happens to everything you believe in?

—Alma in *Persona*

The press conference took place on a spring afternoon in 1966. The scene was a vast studio stage at Svensk Filmindustri in the Stockholm suburb of Räsunda. Seated at a table, Ingmar Bergman and his two stars, Bibi Andersson and Liv Ullmann faced a cadre of reporters anxious to get news of the latest project by Sweden's most famous and most controversial director, a film titled *Persona*. For the most part, Liv and Bibi were silent as Ingmar Bergman tried to answer the reporters' questions. For Liv, introduced to the press in Sweden for the first time, and functioning as the first non-Swedish actress (or actor) ever to appear in a Bergman film, the occasion was not a particularly comfortable one. She had little idea of the specifics of the film. Though she had read the script, she knew that much of the content and all of the technique would materialize as the shooting proceeded. Besides that, she was shy and nervous. But essentially all she had to do was listen as Bergman explained the genesis and the intent of the film.

"This film," Bergman said in response to the first question, "is not connected with the trilogy (*The Virgin Spring*, *Winter Light*, and *Through a Glass Darkly*). It replaces an idea I had previously, because I like this new project very much and I want to do it right away."

Bergman went on to explain that he had gotten the inspiration for *Persona* while he was sick in the hospital, that he had seen Liv Ullmann in a Norwegian film made in 1962 in which Bibi Andersson had also appeared. When the reporters had exhausted all of their questions, the two actresses and the director stood up, ready to leave. The reporters gathered up their briefcases, replaced pens in pockets and shuffled out, mulling over the information they had received. *Persona*, they knew, would be Bergman's twenty-ninth film. Based on his usual schedule, he would shoot in about eight weeks, then spend most of the summer editing what he had shot. It would be released in the fall, and then they would know whether what they had heard was of great or little consequence, whether this would be one of Bergman's lesser or grander efforts. Having gone through a similar routine dozens of times in the past, they were well aware that there was no telling. Sometimes a Bergman film was astounding in its audacity and brilliance, sometimes it was awesome in its private dullness. One thing most of them concluded with certainty: Liv Ullmann was a splendid-looking lady. But if they speculated on Bergman's response to her beauty, it was probably solely in terms of his judgment as a director.

When *Persona* opened in Stockholm on October 18, 1966, the reporters had their answer. Critical praise for the film was overwhelming. *Svenska Dagbladet* described it as "a gripping film" in which Bergman focused on "people who have the same obsessions." The critic of *Expressen* felt it was one of Bergman's simplest, freest and most powerful films, and that it indicated a new power in Bergman, a new direction which was a departure from his previous concentration on religious themes. Other newspapers echoed this praise. The critical conclusion that it was "gripping" and "simple" was high irony indeed, as it would turn out, since critics in other countries more often than not would find *Persona* to be both dull and incomprehensible. All over the world, however, there was no argument with the conclusion that both Bibi Andersson and Liv Ullmann had given magnificent performances, and for the first time in her life, Liv Ullmann would bask in recognition outside of her native land of Norway.

The basic plot of *Persona* is simple and sparse. A famous actress, Elisabet Vogler, played by Liv Ullmann, married and the mother of a boy, elects suddenly to stop speaking. For months she has not uttered a word, but the woman psychiatrist at the hospital where she is being treated cannot find anything mentally of physically wrong with her. A young nurse, Alma, played by Bibi Andersson, is assigned to care for Elisabet. The doctor has a house by the sea to which she sends patient and nurse for a summer's cure. Alma's youthful warmth and solicitude should make Elisabet desire to function again. The summer house becomes the scene of a contest between the women—between the silence of the one and the chatter of the other—which turns from a friendly understanding to a violent and bitter relationship. In the telling of the story, dreams and reality become more and more intertwined. In the end, Alma catches a bus back home by herself. The actress, too, seems to return to the stage, though this is not made totally clear.

Several things greatly complicate the story. There is an elaborate framework of seemingly unrelated—or barely related—images at the beginning and the end, and also, briefly, in the middle of the film. The manner in which the story is told—with sequences that can only be dreams, but without the viewer knowing where the dream begins and ends, or even who is dreaming— creates a confusion of reality and fantasy. There are various duplications, contradictions and unanswered questions. There is an absence of an easily discernible moral scale so that we are not given the usual clues as to how justified an action is. We also do not have the capacity to judge whether a person is sane or not, given the lack of explanation for their actions in the film. We are not sure of the sequence of events, so that our sense of time is disoriented.

Alma and Elisabet seem to stand for innocence and experience, the naïve and the sophisticated. Consider the film's title. *Persona* is the Latin term for a mask, the disguise by which an actor becomes a character. But in psychology, "persona" is the role a human being plays for the benefit of other people, as well as to satisfy the expectations of his own conscious self. And *persona* finally means a person, an individual being. Hence we are to see the film as a dramatic conflict, a movie, but also as a psychic contest between two persons and as the dissection of the interiors of these two persons.

Persona is a Pirandellian kind of work. It is significant that the working title of it was *Film*, and for a long time Bergman refused to distribute stills of the movie unless these photographs had the film camera sprocket markings along the side. In its opening, its middle and its end, Bergman plants clues that are hardly mysterious, but certainly arresting, to make us absorb and reflect on the idea that this *is* a film. We see a quick shot of the camera and cameraman in the course of the opening credits. In the middle of the film, after a particularly climactic moment, the film literally burns up in front of our eyes, then starts up again with the familiar geometric markings that signify the beginning of a reel, and at the end, once more the cameraman appears.

The heart of the film revolves around the impact of Alma and Elisabet on each other. This is seen physically, of course, in their roles as patient and nurse. But it soon becomes psychic and spiritual, as well, as Alma begins to tell Elisabet her innermost thoughts and feelings. And at the midpoint, Bergman even has the two repeat the same speech, an effect that tricked a number of critics, who thought that Alma, who speaks first, was speaking the second time as well. Actually, Elisabet speaks the second time. And then Bergman resorts to what has become the most famous "trick" in the film by subliminally repacing half of Bibi

Andersson's face with the other half of Liv Ullmann's face, so that the composite represents both women.

It is a disturbing and painful image precisely because the two women do look somewhat alike. As a result, the two faces do not look like unrelated forms put together arbitrarily, but like one face—a sick and monstrous one, however—that contradicts itself and wants to split apart again. It is as unsettling as seeing an object—a lamp or a table—straining to disintegrate. What makes the image particularly distressing is that after a while the viewer is not fully aware of what is happening, and the face seen conveys a kind of agony that no face on the screen ever conveyed before. The conclusion must be that the minds behind the faces merge as well, consciously or unconsciously, and that this merging is a terrible, painful thing.

"The subject of *Persona*," Susan Sontag has written, "is the violence of the spirit. If the two women violate each other, each can be said to have at least as profoundly violated herself. In the final parallel to this theme, the film itself seems to be violated—to emerge out of and descend back into the chaos of being 'the cinema.'"

John Simon's interpretation of this complex and elusive film is that Bergman is offering apologies in the film for his treatment of "certain women he has been involved with, from whom he took more than he gave, only to end up immersing himself in his work while they were left helpless, fists beating against a locked door. Though the egocentric male lover is disguised as the woman patient, the relationship between Alma and Elisabet has manifestly erotic, passionate characteristics. This is true both of their highly charged hostilities and of their psychic fusion. Strindberg commented on the phenomenon of "doubles" in love: "We begin to love a woman by depositing with her our souls, bit by bit. We duplicate our personality; and the beloved woman who formerly was indifferent and neutral begins to assume the guise of our other self, becoming our double." The conflict in *Persona* is an aspect of a larger conflict, the battle of the sexes, as it keeps appearing in Strindberg—and in Bergman. The form it usually takes is the humiliation of one lover by the other, and this is precisely what happens in *Persona*, as Alma finally revolts against Elisabet's domination of her. And while she was making the film, Liv Ullmann was convinced that Elisabet represented Ingmar Bergman.

Shortly after the film was released, Bergman and Liv confirmed what rumor and gossip was imagining by issuing a statement from the island, where they were living in Bergman's $100,000 stone and glass house, with its polished wood floors, wool rugs and natural-wood furniture, all so much a reflection of the Scandinavian style. Both began divorce proceedings against their spouses, but the divorces were far from final when Liv gave birth to her daughter Linn. The scandal that exploded was fueled by the fact that the couple maintained that they saw no necessity for them to be married even after they had been divorced.

Recalling these events some seven years later, Liv said: "I fell in love with Ingmar while we were making the film. My husband and I had five good years together, but the marriage had failed. I saw later that I had expected my husband to give me the marriage. I thought that marriage was made to serve me, make me happy, and give me a husband who protected and took care of me. I learned that it should be something between two equal human beings who help and guide each other. It can't be good when the woman is some sort of clinging flower who sits waiting for her man to bring happiness home."

This judgment came after she and Ingmar Bergman had parted in 1971. Characteristically, the break came with Bergman vainly fighting publicity over it. The only "personal" statement he had ever made in 1969 about his love for Liv was, "As in photography, Liv is a complete commentary unto herself. Besides, I am in love with her—creatively and personally." The breakup came as Bergman was giving a rare series of interviews to Swedish journalist Maud Wester, which appeared in a Swedish magazine, *Vecko Jouranlen*, in Stockholm. On television, after the interviews were over, Bergman complained that his privacy was being invaded because journalists were assuming that since Liv had gone to Denmark, taking Linn with her, there was trouble in their household. This, said Bergman, was utter nonsense; she had simply gone shopping. A week later, the official word came: the famous couple had separated. They never got together again, except as director and actress. Liv herself has said that the break came at Bergman's initiative. When she went away, she did expect to come back again, but then she received a "Dear Liv" letter from Bergman explaining that he felt they should part.

In her relationship with Bergman, Liv was assuredly not the "equal" she referred to in 1972. Far more than her first husband, Bergman was undoubtedly the fantasy father she created as a child. "To me," she said in 1972, "he was God. I admired him so much, and I was twenty-five—too young—and he was forty-six. When he spoke, I blushed. I remember that he was worried the first week of shooting *Persona*. But he trusts the people he picks, and the moment you open up, he will be there, and he was in that instance, too."

Often married—four times when he met Liv—

Bergman seems to draw new strength and youth from each of his affairs. With Liv as his star and companion, he moved into a new creative phase. His pictures became less theological, less concerned with God, man, and the devil, and more concerned with people, especially women. This trend, of course, culminated in *Scenes from a Marriage*. Yet, if Bergman uses women, they gain at least as much from him. Liv now feels that Bergman gave her "much more self-confidence than I ever had before. He listened to me. Living with him enriched me. I matured. The world I lived in with my husband was much smaller, mostly of neighbors and close friends. With Ingmar's friends, I had to sharpen up and find my own identity."

When Liv became pregnant, it was no surprise to her. "I let it happen," she says. "I wasn't afraid. I felt it was very right." Linn was born during the filming of *Hour of the Wolf*. Exercising her professional curiosity, Liv took careful note of her own cries and groans during the birth, cataloging them for future use if she ever played a woman in labor.

It was the harassment of her Norwegian compatriots that Liv neglected to calculate when she decided to have a baby with Bergman. In much the same way that Ingrid Bergman was castigated and reviled when she gave birth to Roberto Rossellini's children, Liv was subjected to denunciation that was on the incredible side, considering the supposed advance of sexual freedom in the intervening years. Hundred of letters arrived on Färo, the gist of all of them that she was a sinful woman, a whore who would receive her just punishment for the awful crime against morality that she had committed. Some letters announced that if the sender were in her shoes, he or she would take the baby into the woods and leave it. Others graciously suggested that she should kill herself as well. That kind of public reaction can be strengthening, once one gets over the sinking feeling that the world is really quite full of very strange people. Liv wanted the child christened in the protestant church to which she herself belonged, but the Norwegian church flatly refused to do so, and nothing changed this, even if Liv felt so frustrated that she appeared in the Norwegian TV, where she, deeply moved, tried to defend herself. That she felt compelled to do this, in spite of being fundamentally shy, shows how heavy the blow was, and how deeply she was affected by it. Liv is quite convinced that she behaved morally and honestly by not marrying Bergman. Whether a marriage might have prevented the break between them or not is of course an open question, but the answer will probably be no, considering that Bergman had not minded divorcing his four previous wives.

In Sweden the uproar over the affair was considerably less. The Swedes had a much more liberal attitude towards morals, but instead they were recklessly curious to see Liv "at home"—and no matter if the couple was at Farö or in Bergman's expensive house in Stockholm's suburb Djurgarden, they often were under siege of inquisitive people.

Liv was not quite happy on Farö from the beginning, the bleak loneliness of the place made her feel cut off from things. In the past, Bergman had found this isolation to be a great advantage in his relationship with a woman. "When a girlfriend and I quarrel," he noted, "and she wants to go away and she is all packed, everything is always too complicated. First she has to drive a very complicated way through the woods. Then the ferry boat leaves only on the hour. From there, she has to find a flight. So she ends up staying."

For a long time, as we know, Liv ended up staying,

too. Not that there were earth-shattering quarrels. On the contrary, much of the time they spent together on the island was occupied with filmmaking, and Liv was enthralled to be a member of Bergman's acting company as well as to be his companion. But on the island or in Stockholm, Bergman is an extremely private person in the sense that he values his time immensely and guards it with a vengeance. He loathes parties and sees only old friends and people with whom he is working on stage film or TV prjects. He is not at all intrigued with the idea of travel, both because it would take him away from his work—he has said that he will never make a movie outside of Sweden—and because he seems to feel uncomfortable in new places and with new people.

At one point in their life together, however, he was contemplating a joint project with Federico Fellini, and Liv and Bergman went to Rome together on a combined holiday and business trip. In Rome, Bergman was very much the proverbial fish out of water, seemingly terrified at getting entangled in the problems that a strange city can throw up to a visitor who doesn't speak the language. Consequently, Liv could rarely budge him from their hotel room, and he insisted on returning every day to the first restaurant they had tried. Strange behavior for a man not loath to go way out on limbs as a filmmaker. However, as timid as he was in his confrontation with Rome, he remained aggressive in his relationship with Liv, insisting on ordering for both of them at every meal.

Liv's idea of life with Bergman was highly conventional. She was undoubtedly still not over her first conception of love and living together as a situation which, as she said, "was made to serve me, make me happy and give me a husband [or man] who protected and took care of me." And above all, she wanted security of a special kind, the security of entrusting her emotions to a man and not being hurt by him when she did so. She envisioned their life together as a series of scenes in which they would walk arm in arm down the lane, pushing the baby carriage; sit in front of the fire, dreamily sipping wine; skip hand in hand over a meadow on a bright, sunny day. This, was not the way it turned out. Bergman was not interested in wheeling a baby carriage, and while he was far from the dour, sour gentlemen that many accounts would make him out to be—he is actually full of vitality, likes to laugh and joke, often highly playful—he was something of a "workaholic," and therefore not as available for Liv as she wanted him to be.

All of this turned Liv back again to the unconfident schoolgirl she was trying to outgrow. She became highly insecure about her situation in the household. "I was running from one room to the next, feeling bad all the time, feeling I was neglecting the baby or the nanny or the dog or Ingmar. When I was with one, I thought the others were unhappy. Never did I do what I wanted to do. That is something I learned from Ingmar. He is not afraid to do what he wants to do."

It was, no doubt, a case of inflated expectations on Liv's part pitted against the commonsense attitude toward one's beloved that a man who has had four wives would naturally have grown into on Bergman's part. If, in every relationship between a man and a woman, one or the other is more secure, more sure that he or she has the upper hand, that the other is afraid of not pleasing; then Liv was clearly the one who was the less secure.

When things became unstable enough for them to talk about breaking up, they arranged a three-month trial separation. Liv took Linn and went to Denmark, then back to Norway. They talked nightly on the phone, sometimes for as long as two hours. Liv finally told Bergman that she wanted to come back. He responded cordially but vaguely, and soon Liv received the good-bye letter from him.

The breakup was a terrible nightmare for Liv. "It was so public," she recalls. "I felt that everyone was looking at me. I don't know where you can hide your sorrows anymore." Scandal magazines and newspapers hounded her—Bergman is big news in Scandinavia, and this was a juicy story—and reporters and photographers followed her wherever she went. One day, to get away from them, friends took her out the back door of a Copenhagen hotel, leaving her for a minute in an alley while they went to find a cab. "I was standing there in the garbage," Liv remembers, "and I felt it was so symbolic. Something died in me. I resolved I would never let that happen to me again." Yet, at the same time, her instinct as an artist made her examine her reactions minutely and made her feel that the experience would be of benefit to her. "I was crying floods of tears, and I would think: 'This makes me grow as an artist.'"

Having gone through something of a crucible in her experience with Bergman, Liv now has much more definite ideas of what she wants from a man. Asked if she still nurtures the thought of an enduring relationship, she says, rather testily, "What do you think I feel when I am alone in my room, when there is nobody there? I am very lonely. I want to be in somebody's pocket, to be taken care of." She stops and shakes her head, letting her blonde hair swirl around her like leaves in a sudden gust of wind. "But then I want to be free, too." And it is the last statement that tells the story of Liv's experience with Bergman, for she is no longer the girl who dreams of absolute comfort with a man;

she is now an independent creature who knows that she must pursue her art at the same time that she pursues someone who can "put her in his pocket," and if there is a conflict, it's a good bet that art will win out. That was the Bergman formula, and it's another thing that Liv picked up from him.

"What I need from a man," she reflects, "is that he must love me. When I tell him that I want to quit acting and stay home and cook dinners, he must immediately say no. Because he should know that it is as a working woman that I am happy and can make him happy. He must believe that our relationship is forever and work for it, just as I want to believe it and work for it. And if it is not forever, then he must not be that sort of hateful person who will be inflamed at a breakup."

As for her final appraisal of her relationship with Bergman, enough time has passed so that Liv can view what happened with an equanimity that is hard-earned. "If we had stayed together," she says, "we wouldn't have been good for each other for the rest of our lives. We still have what was best or most of what was best. We are friends and we work together. What was bad was that we limited each other. We were both strong and so much alike that we canceled each other out. And because I was the younger, I canceled myself out more and tried to live his life—which was natural enough. Then I had a revelation about this and, in the end, I was fighting so hard that I didn't make him happy. I think he needs an entirely different kind of person to live with. He needs other things than I could give. His present wife lives for him and nothing else. He is her great ambition, her love, everything. And I think that's what he needs because he has all the rest. He is very close to a few friends, and, obviously, very, very close to his work. So things other men have to find in marriage he gets elsewhere. Then he has somebody at home who really cares for him. She writes his letters, types his scripts, answers the telephone for him, arranges his business meetings and copes with his finances.

"I think because of what I have been through, I feel safer not marrying again. Because I'd hate to be divorced twice. I'm too dramatic. I'd feel it was an awful admission of failure. Marriage is so complicated. You live together for five or ten years; then you marry and the next day it's hell. It's like you suddenly own the other person and have the right to be callous and lazy. But if it's a good relationship, I don't think marriage really hurts. It's a lovely thing to have a ceremony together, to promise something together in a ceremony. You don't love each other more or do more for each other because you are married. But I think we all need a little manifestation because we are a little insecure."

André Malraux once wrote: "A lover possesses only those things that he's changed in the one he loves." On that basis, it would be hard to say what Ingmar Bergman possesses of Liv Ullmann. Perhaps she made him more conscious of the kind of women he really needs, hence the happiness of his present marriage. And perhaps she made him more conscious of how tenuous the line between love and domination can be. As for what she possesses of Bergman, certainly a stronger feeling for her destiny as an artist, perhaps an experience of defeat which Bergman, through many years of critical condemnation, gradually learned to live with, though in his youth what the critics said was as painful to him as a knife wound.

Whatever the balance sheet, however, it is fair to say

that this relationship, which began with a film about doubles, about the interaction of two people, both physically and psychically, was a case of life imitating art. Bergman had always had the feeling of guilt induced by denying yourself to another (or that part of yourself you know the other wants). Long before he met Liv, he had experienced the pangs of guilt in his relationships with other women, as his demon to work drove him further from them.

It was ironic for Liv that the first picture she made with Bergman explored the very experience that she would have with him in their life together. Playing the role of Elisabet, Liv brought to it a marvelous instinct for a character whose life experience was far from her own. Without dialogue to speak, she managed to convey a wonderfully broad range of feeling, to create a real person. It was only later, as she experienced what Bergman had to offer her, that she absorbed the actual raw material on which the role of Elisabet was based in Bergman's own mind.

As Berman has said, "I always write with particular actors in mind. My actors are all on the stage constantly and it makes such a difference, this daily contact with a director. They can do almost instinctively what I want. Yet they're not slaves, they're always themselves, always a little different from the way I imagined them." How Bergman imagined Liv to be is an interesting question. He had, after all, seen her only in one Norwegian film, made some years before he wrote *Persona*. Obviously, on the set of *Persona*, her reality became much larger than he'd imagined it in terms of the film, so large that it overwhelmed him.

The further fascinating element in their odyssey together is the effect it had on his work. It is safe to say that had it not been for his time with Liv, *Scenes from a Marriage* would be an entirely different film. As Bergman was preparing the script for *Scenes*, Liv was quoted as saying: "Bergman is now starting to create a sort of new woman character, a woman who's really free and who can live without the help and support of a man." And yet Liv is quick to deny that *Scenes* is really about her and Bergman. "There are very few moments," she says, "where I would say, 'This really happened.' But there are parallel experiences which I had with him and with other people, things I know he has heard from other people. And I recognize scenes from other marriages both of us know. And some of it comes out of his head. But it's not the autobiography of our relationship—far from it."

And yet, while this is literally true, it is also true that the impulse for the character, a woman who frees herself from her own weaknesses, undoubtedly came, in large part, from Liv herself.

CHAPTER SIX

The Real Liv

Love is more important than the job. You throw yourself into a job when you can't do other things. But deep down we want to talk about the human condition ... it's about a relationship and a longing for it, so that even people who have never had one can understand it.

—Liv Ullmann speaking about
Scenes from a Marriage

There's the sprawling $300,000 house and, of course, the gleaming pool. There are also the rolling lawns and the lush gardens, the lovely Hawaiian lanai, the neat well-stocked patio. And sitting amidst this Beverly Hills splendor is Liv Ullmann, whom Hollywood believes will rank in the pantheon alongside Greta Garbo and Ingrid Bergman.

She is in Hollywood to sing and dance in the $8,000,000 movie musical, *Lost Horizon*. Though admittedly she sings a bit off-key and she keeps telling all who will listen seriously that she is on the clumsy side, director Charles Jarrott is unconcerned. He believes firmly that she will be sensational in the film.

Later in 1972, she will do another film in Hollywood—*Forty Carats*—a role so highly coveted by the leading ladies of the movie colony that even Liz Taylor, Joanne Woodward and Julie Christie—three who could presumably have their pick of parts—went out on a limb and declared their passion to be chosen.

Liv is in the midst of a sudden wave of popularity. Across America, she can be seen in no less than four different films: *Cries and Whispers, Pope Joan, The Settlers*, and *The Emigrants*. She is in fact the hottest new actress around, and this of course is the reason that Hollywood wanted her so desperately for *Lost Horizon*. She has done nothing like this film, a typical studio remake of a classic success which brought Ronald Colman total stardom some thirty years ago into a 1970s "joyful and tuneful musical extravaganza," but Hollywood is convinced that her "star quality" will carry the day and turn the film into the hoped-for bonanza, the commercial success that the brilliance of the score and the presence of the aging Charles Boyer and Peter Finch, a solid, sometimes even brilliant actor who has never been able to carry the day at the box office, would not alone be sufficient to produce.

Perhaps Liv feels uneasy about what she's let herself in for. At any rate, on a day in August, sitting by her pool, she is telling a newspaperman that she does not feel comfortable in these sybaritic surroundings. "I'm easily ashamed by such excesses," she says, nodding her head in the direction of the oversized house and tailored shrubbery and lawns. "If I lived here all the time, I'd be continually embarrassed by this big house, the luxurious cars and everything else. Nobody has things like this in Norway. It's a strict socialist country, and no one is supposed to own so much. If I drove a big car, it would be impossible for me to be happy in Norway. My friends wouldn't like me anymore. Of course, I have more than the average in Norway, a lot more than the average Norwegian woman—a house and a small car. But everyone has that here."

Liv has made a number of friends in the movie colony, and ordinarily would be extremely happy. But the smell of money which she senses pervading everything in town does not sit well with her.

"Actors are grossly overpaid in America," she says, reaching for a soft drink sitting on a wrought-iron table at the edge of the pool. "I think it can harm a performer to get so much money for what he does. But still, the actors I've met are really very nice, very friendly and generous. Sometimes I feel it doesn't really come from the heart, but still, it makes life pleasant. Just so they smile—that's one less thing to worry about. But inside myself, I feel strongly that people in Norway are more honest than here. Of course, they are maybe not so contented with their life, so that's another problem."

Beverly Hills astounds Liv. "I don't understand why you never see anyone on the streets," she says, giggling as though this fact were part of some great mystery that will never be solved. There's never anyone at the windows of houses, either. All there are are lots of cars. Sometimes I think there's no one in the cars, either, that they are just driving around by remote control." She giggles again, knowing very well that she is being playful and enjoying the role. "But what disturbs me, really, is that if all these people don't *do* anything, just stay in their closets, maybe, and look at all they have, all this richness, all these beautiful green lawns and swimming pools. The other day my daughter was playing in front of the house and a policeman came by and saw her and knocked on the door. 'You'd better take her inside,' he told me, 'a car might grab her.' Imagine that! A child can't even play on the lawn in this place."

The Beverly Hills style of life really does not appeal to her. Perhaps it's a conflict between the directness of her Norwegian soul and her commitment to "honesty" in life and in her career as an actress and what seems to be the furtiveness and fearfulness of the local residents. "The other day," she relates, "I was driving into town about seven o'clock in the evening and we happened to see a man walking down the street. A totally ordinary man, the only thing even *identifying* about him that I could see was that he was wearing thick eyeglasses. But my friend immediately drove to the police station and reported that this 'suspicious' fellow was out there. God knows what he was going to do. I was really totally shocked. You can't even take a walk in this place without becoming an object of suspicion."

In Norway, Liv explains, she loves to walk. "On Sunday in particular," she says, "everyone hikes up to the mountains. Well, almost everyone," smiling at her small penchant for exaggeration, which, it is evident, is based on a desire to please and charm. "But I've stopped walking here because no one else does, and I wouldn't want to get reported to the police as a suspicious character, would I?"

She reaches down to smooth her stomach through the thin peasant-style blouse she's wearing, then runs her hand down bare tanned thighs. "It's a bad habit, getting into the car everytime you want to go someplace. I even do it now just to go to the post office, two blocks away, and I think it's beginning to show.

I've gained five pounds since I've been here, and I blame it all on nonexercise and Chinese food. I happen to be crazy about Chinese food, chow mein and all those other delights. We have only two Chinese restaurants back in Norway, and they're quite ordinary, really—not at all as good as the ones here. So when I go to one, I tend to be a little crazy, and I seem to go to one every time I eat out."

Though she walks a lot in Norway, Liv doesn't do much else in the way of exercise, but that fact doesn't seem to faze her at all, an attitude that marks her, among others, as being quite apart from the normal Beverly Hills lady, whose concern for her athletic ability amounts to an obsession, particularly in the case of the latest craze—tennis. Liv is aware of this, but characteristically would no more think of adjusting herself to local conditions than she would of living in California for any length of time. On her first trip, when she came to Hollywood in the spring of 1971 to accept Ingmar Bergman's Oscar for *Cries and Whispers* as the best foreign film of the year, she took a good look around but felt no great desire to stay. She might have been tempted had she been approached in any way about the possibility of doing a film, but not a word was said at that time, and back to Norway she went, telling herself that it was undoubtedly true that she was not "the Hollywood type," whatever that might be. Having convinced herself that this was true, and feeling a tinge of regret at not being given the opportunity to explore this new scene, she found herself with quite mixed feelings when the producer of *Lost Horizon*, Blake Edwards, got in touch with her and asked her to star in the film.

Amazement was her first reaction. "I couldn't understand why they chose me. I told them I wasn't a great singer. They said, 'We'll work it out.' I told them I was really not very graceful, especially on the dance floor. I never like to get up and dance because I'm so awkward. They said, 'Don't worry about it.' Finally I told them that outside of having sung on stage in a Brecht play, I had never done a musical. All my experience has been with serious dramatic works. They just said, 'You'll be fantastic.'"

As if that wasn't amazing enough, shortly after she arrived in Hollywood, the producer of *Forty Carats*, Mike Frankovich, called her and said: "We want you for this film." Liv knew the play and thought that Frankovich was talking about the role of the teen-age daughter, which doubly amazed her, since at thirty-two, though she felt she looked young, she did not think she could get away with playing a teen-ager. Just when she was about to tell him that she couldn't consider that role, he offered her the role of the mother, who is in her early forties. Having looked at the script, Liv then accepted that part. "The screenplay is much more serious than the stage version, and I really feel close to the woman I'll portray," she says.

Frankovich's desire to feature Liv in this film was understandable. There are few producers in the world and few directors who wouldn't have considered it a coup to have Liv in a film at this point. What excites Liv most about the prospect of these two films is the change of pace. "I've always appeared in sad, tragic stories on stage and screen," she says. "The switch to comedy and a musical represents a fantastic change for me. I feel as if I'm going to have whole new life to live."

She thinks back now to her early childhood, when even at age seven, she knew she wanted to be an actress. "I wasn't very charming as a child," she says now, thoughtfully, "but I always got attention. And I learned that the way to do it was through acting. Later I discovered that it was a way to make people laugh and cry, and I liked that."

With her relationship to Bergman behind her, Liv

still thinks about marriage, but she's in no rush to get married again, and often she leans to the view that she may never get married again. "Once you have promised yourself to a man in front of an altar, you hesitate about doing it again. It's a religious thing with me. I happen to believe in God but don't go to church. The marriage license is meaningless. I believe two people can live happily together without being married."

Though acting represents Liv's major means of expressing herself, she also writes. "When I feel lost, I'll sit down in front of the typewriter. I've written several essays that have been published in the newspapers back in Norway. And I fully intend to write one on Hollywood when I get back home."

One thing her stay in Hollywood has given her the chance to do is see some American films, and what she's seen has not particularly pleased her. She thinks the emphasis on nudity is definitely the wrong track. "I think," she says, "that it's really a lot of crap when directors tell actresses they should go naked because the script requires it. Most films could be done just as well without naked bodies. I remember a scene from a French film, *The Lovers,* in which Jeanne Moreau and an actor were making love. All you saw were two hands meeting. To me it was much more sensual than an actual closeup of two bodies."

As for Liv, she has never peeled off her clothes in any of her twenty-five films, and she doesn't intend to. "I feel your private life is more important than showing off everything. Once you are naked on film, what have you left for someone you care about? You have to give away so much of yourself anyway as an actress, I think you have to draw the line somewhere, and right now I believe it's best for me to draw it at nudity." And yet, it seems safe to say, if a film came along that absolutely required Liv to present herself naked on the screen because the script demanded it, she would not hesitate a minute to do it. It's safe to say this because, in any role she has ever played, she has revealed herself to the fullest extent the script demanded, and nudity would be no exception.

One film that literally astounded Liv was *Prime Cut,* which in truth does shape up as a raunchy and silly example of Hollywood's current fascination with unclothed bodies—female, mainly—designed to be the commodity that will compete with the porno industry's much greater output. "I never saw anything like it," Liv says of *Prime Cut,* a statement which simply proves that she's never seen a porno film. "That movie was the worst I've ever seen. How could Lee Marvin and Gene Hackman have permitted themselves to be seen in it? Surely they must have read the script?" The answer, of course, is money.

Reading scripts is something that Liv feels very strongly about. She insists that before she takes a role, she must see something that approximates fairly closely the final shooting script. "Of course, an actor can be totally wrong about how a film will turn out and, perhaps less so about the specific dimensions of his own role. But still, you must think about these things beforehand. In my case, what I look for is the quality of the project. And then I must get the feeling that my own particular role is *me.* I don't mean that in an absolute sense, of course, but I have to feel a stirring in my blood, I have to feel that the woman I'm going to play is, somehow, *related* to me."

Hollywood life will be over for Liv early in the spring, and then she will be going back to Europe, first to make another film with Bergman, then to go back on the stage again. The role this time will be as the star of Brecht's *The Good Woman of Szechuan,* and both her role as "the good woman" and the play itself seem very right and demanding to her. She is not at all concerned that she will be working for something like one-fiftieth of her movie salary, and instead of being involved in a project that will receive worldwide attention, as *Lost Horizon* and *Forty Carats* will, she will be ensconced in the relative backwater of Norway. "Basically I'm a stage actress," she says, "and I feel that it's very important for me to keep watering those roots. Anyway, my daughter will be starting school next year and my time will be limited because of that. I want to be with my daughter, so I can't go traveling all over the place."

Just then, Linn dashes across the lawn and without a glance at Liv or her interviewer, dives straight into the pool. She swims effortlessly, an art she learned just a few months ago. Dripping water and totally self-absorbed she surfaces at the side of the pool, climbs the ladder out and dives right in again. She repeats this maneuver for the next five minutes, and it is an excellent example of a child auditioning for a part in a water follies. Is she, like her mother before her, totally enamored of the opportunity to perform? She isn't talking about that. But Liv is becoming concerned at this theatrical swimming exhibition, and finally she manages to catch Linn coming out and before she can dive in again. She pulls the girl close to her and says, "Have you gone Hollywood, Linn?"

Maybe Linn has, but she shakes her head "no."

That's all Liv can fasten on at the moment, and she says, "That's good. I haven't either."

It's three o'clock on a Saturday afternoon. Outside the rain floods the New York streets, making the sky dark and the scene bleak and uninviting. It is November 10, 1972, six months past the pool and the tailored lawns of Beverly Hills. But there's something of Beverly Hills inside the Plaza Hotel, that Rennaissance pile squatting off Fifth Avenue. In the marbled lobby, klieg lights are bathing the scene in a brilliance that rivals the California sunshine. Even the potted palms look West Coast instead of suffering Manhattan indoor greenery. A huge camera on rollers moves in to record the scene. The lobby is crowded with two sets of people, the actors in a film that's being shot, and a good handful of curious observers who are allowed to watch the goings-on by the film people as long as they don't do anything crazy, like ask for an autograph in the middle of the scene, or try to become instant stars by running in front of the camera, or even talk loudly to a friend as the scene is being shot. Good behavior is required, but the policing is necessarily on the scanty side, and there is a lot of murmuring, a lot of oohs and ahs and "look at that" as the proceedings unfold.

Standing shyly off in a corner of the crowd a lady with a radiant smile and a charming Scandinavian accent is approached by two women shoppers who are not being policed and have no intention of obeying the "silence, please" refrain being mouthed by an assistant director.

"Excuse me, please," says one of the shoppers, tugging at the lady's sleeve. "What's going on here?"

"They're making a movie," says the lady with the accent.

"Which one?" the other shopper asks.

"It's called *Forty Carats*," the lady says.

"Oh, it's *Forty Carats*," the second shopper tells the first, as if the first were not almost standing on her shoulder and well able to hear the reply.

Then, turning back to the lady with the accent, she says: "Who's in it?"

"Well," the patient lady replies, "I'm the star."

"Really?" the shopper says. "May I ask who you are?"

"Liv Ullmann."

"Well, it's nice to meet you," the first and less aggressive shopper says, and then the two ladies move off.

As they pause at the lobby's revolving door, Liv Ullmann can hear one say to the other, "Who's Liv Ullmann?"

To which the reply is, "Search me, I never heard of her. It must not be much of a movie."

At that point, you couldn't really take the ladies to task for their lack of knowledge. And, in fact, you could have congratulated one of them on her powers of prognostication, because, no fault of Liv Ullmann's, *Forty Carats* would turn out to be "not much of a movie." But that would come later. For now, the publicity mills on the West Coast were in full, booming operation, trying to tell lady shoppers and all others who could be made to listen just who Liv Ullmann was, and just why *Forty Carats* would repeat the resounding success it had had as a Broadway hit, when it loomed at you from silver screens all across the country. The problem was that despite the four movies she had been seen in during the past year, Liv Ullmann was still not a household word in America, unless the household made it a practice to see Ingmar Bergman movies.

But the feeling of the men in Hollywood who had their fingers on the pulse of America clearly was that this ignorance would not last very long. *Lost Horizon* would be released in a few months, it was destined to be one of those "big" movies that Hollywood is always shooting for but seldom produces, and then everyone would know who Liv Ullmann was, and in the star-studded cast of that extravaganza, she would outshine the likes of Charles Boyer, Peter Finch, John Gielgud, and Michael York.

That was why Liv had been chosen for the starring role in *Forty Carats* after every other possibility had been turned down. And the bandwagon was really rolling along now, the hoopla generating more hoopla in the best showbiz tradition, for Liv now had three more films to be made in Hollywood in the next couple of years after she finished *Forty Carats*. Hollywood's wise men knew a good thing when they saw one, knew that Ross Hunter and Mike Frankovich couldn't be wrong, and they wanted in on the killing.

"Listen," Leonard Gershe, the author of the *Forty Carats* screenplay told a leading movie critic as the film was being made, "everybody wanted to do this film. Audrey Hepburn, Joanne Woodward, Doris Day, Elizabeth Taylor. It's a great role. A forty-year-old woman in love with her daughter's twenty-one-year-old boyfriend. I had never seen her on the screen. I've only seen two Ingmar Bergman films in my life, and she wasn't in either one of them. Then one day I was talking to Richard Avedon, the photographer, who had just shot her for *Vogue* magazine, and he went on and on about how exciting she was and so I went to see her in a couple of films and I knew she was the one."

Gershe could hardly contain his excitement. "She is an incredible actress," he said. "Wait until you see her in this film. She is sensational. And Mike Frankovich likes unknowns. Look what he did for Goldie Hawn in *Butterflies Are Free*. Of course, I had to change some of the elements in the play. It was much more of a French farce as a play, because it started out in France as a French farce. In the film you don't see them in bed. They do it on the beach, in a sleeping bag. It won't be a picture for the children. Yes, she gets the younger man in the end. The daughter gets the older man. Just like in real life." He laughed at this witticism. "But seriously," he said, "it's a serious story now, not just an empty comedy."

Gershe could speak with the authority of success. The same team that had made his play, *Butterflies are Free* into a smash movie, was together again to tune

Forty Carats down the same road. There was producer Mike Frankovich, Gershe as the screenwriter, Milton Katselas to direct, cinematographer Charles Land, and Edward Albert to costar with Liv as he had costarred with Goldie Hawn.

All of them say that Liv is a most delicious person. "A happy Swede, that's what she is," says the wardrobe lady. "Who ever heard of such a thing?" Informed that Liv was from Norway, not Sweden, the wardrobe lady is undeterred. "It's the same thing," she says. "They're two countries right next to each other, and everyone knows that's not a happy part of the world. It must be the cold and the fog." But if the wardrobe lady's sense of national character is a bit on the foggy side, her powers of observation are real enough, and she's been in the business long enough to know a winner from a loser. Liv Ullmann is a winner in her book. "She's like Ingrid Bergman," the wardrobe lady goes on. A cliché from an early thirties movie about Broadway, she is short, portly, always wears shapeless black dresses, and has a band of freckles across her pug nose. "She's very, very together," the wardrobe lady concludes. "And when she acts, let me tell you, there isn't a dry eye on the set."

Since wardrobe ladies have as good an average in choosing stars as the best producers, it seems that Liv Ullmann is a terrific bet for stardom.

Now, in the Plaza lobby, the crew clears the set for the final take on the scene. It's from the end of the film. Liv has agreed to marry the boy. His parents are told and they come to New York to meet her. She's supposed to face them in the company of the boy, but she purposely arrives early, wanting to satisfy some unmanageable doubt she still has about the whole thing, and the parents turn out to be very tough, very unyielding. Their son has his whole life ahead of him, so why should he marry a forty-year-old? Totally destroyed by this confrontation, which seems, indeed, to echo—if not confirm—her very own fears and doubts, Liv will come out of the elevator pursued by Edward Albert (who has arrived in the middle of the dogfight with the parents, but has not been able to restore Liv's composure), still trying to convince her that everything will be all right. "Wait," he shouts as he runs across the patterned carpet after Liv, "I've never been so sure of anything in my life."

Liv's face has fallen apart, her eyes are red-rimmed, or so it seems, not from crying, but from holding tears back. To one who has seen rushes of the hotel room fight, she is a lot more convincing running away from the boy than she was facing the parents and trying to convince them—and more importantly, herself—that the idea of their marriage makes some sense. In fact, this will turn out to be the fatal flaw in the film, because as it's written, for the motivations given, and with the characters set as they are, there is no conviction in the idea that Liv Ullmann is the woman for this boy.

But Liv is far from aware of this at the Plaza, and after the director signals that's he's happy with the lobby take, Liv goes off with an interviewer to the Palm Court. There, at a tiny marble-topped table, she has an espresso, and talks about the film, and her status as a movie star in America. "I think people will know me very well soon because *Lost Horizon* and *Forty Carats* are good films and they will do well, I think. Now, of course, they can't know me, because after all I was only in a lot of Bergman films that not so many people see. You know," she says, becoming even more serious, and gazing intently out of her extraordinarily blue eyes at the interviewer, "Bergman makes only *serious* movies, and that is another reason I am not so well known, because people don't always want to be serious, they want to be entertained, and often they go to the movies for exactly this reason, to laugh or even to cry but not in a serious way, because they know the problem is only in the movie. But Bergman makes films that connect with real life, and when you cry at a Bergman film, it's because you are crying for yourself, for real, because you see how the movie is about you, or about real people and real problems.

"In Bergman movies, I always play a very serious character. I always play the girl who gets killed or the woman whose husband doesn't love her or tries to leave her. And the same onstage. I've always wanted to play comedy; Bergman always said I should play comedy, but he never gave me anything to play. So it is ironic that I should come to America to have this chance, because after all, I've made twenty-five films in Europe, and this is only my second American film; and no American producer has ever seen me do comedy, so it is really hard to understand how this has happened, but anyway, it has and I'm very happy about it."

Then Liv explains how she came to be in Hollywood when Mike Frankovich and Ross Hunter asked her to star for them. "I came to do publicity for *The Emigrants*," she says. "It was nominated for an Oscar last year, you know, and I arrived in Hollywood with one small suitcase because I planned to stay for only ten days. Then someone suggested that I see Ross Hunter about the part in *Lost Horizon*. He probably thought I was very neurotic, so he didn't want me for the part at first. But the director, Charles Jarrott, who directed *Mary, Queen of Scots*, talked him into seeing me, and I guess he liked me. I don't know why." She pauses, replaying the scene in her mind. And then she confirms that she is still growing into the role of the Hollywood star, a role in which one's value is so self-evident that most of the lines that are uttered involve an explanation of how complicated life is coping with fame, by saying, her eyes going off to the corner of the room, "I didn't tell him jokes or anything."

Now that she's out of Hollywood after something like a five-month stay, she knows for sure that it is not the place for her to live. Working is another matter, of course. "As soon as the film [*Lost Horizon*] was over, I went back to Sweden to make another film for Bergman on a deserted island with no drinking water, where you have to walk almost a mile to an outside toilet. It was more fulfilling to me than doing *Lost Horizon*. And after *Forty Carats* I will go home again. I could 'go Hollywood,' as they say, but I don't like it there. I still don't know how to get anywhere on the freeways."

The film that Liv Ullmann went back to make between *Lost Horizon* and *Forty Carats* was *Scenes from a Marriage*, and in the wonderful but totally fickle world of films, it was this film not the previous two which would make her the star that Hollywood hoped she would become. After six Bergman films, numerous stage plays in Norway and eight non-Bergman films, six of them Hollywood-made, Liv Ullmann was an international film star of the first magnitude, but not the towering-figure she would become after the release of *Scenes from a Marriage*. She was not yet a cult figure who was, besides being the successor to Greta Garbo and Ingrid Bergman, the world's most glamourous and gifted actress, but also a representative of the new woman of women's lib, the women of achievement and talent. Not a pawn of the man's world but an independent, self-reliant and true-to-her-soul real woman that millions of other women could admire and try to emulate precisely because she had combined the capture of success with the capture of her own self. Here was no Marilyn Monroe, who mouthed lines she thought would bring her success, enhance her "image," make her even more of a commodity for men—producers or voyeurs—to diddle about as they desired, and whether she realized it or not, all for their own profit at the expense of her soul. Here was a woman who said and did what she thought she should, not for profit, not for image aggrandizement, but because it was good for her self, that center of her being that, as she often explained, she had been trying to perfect, as millions of other women were trying to perfect theirs, since she had been an awkward and shy teen-ager.

It was *Scenes from a Marriage* that projected for the first time this image of Liv Ullmann to the world. True, it was on the screen, it was a film, not real life. But the audience perceived an enormously strong aura of reality in this performance. It was, the audience felt, "authentic." And as is often the case, the audience was quite correct. There were two levels to this perception. One was that Liv Ullmann played the part so "honestly" that her playing must reflect the core of her own personality. The second was that, if by some masterpiece of dissembling, Liv Ullmann was indeed in real life something approaching a Marilyn Monroe, it didn't matter a bit, because the performance was so strong, so good, and so right for the mood of a world trying to reconcile the aggressiveness of women's lib to the job of getting along with the woman you took out to dinner, that even if Liv Ullmann was the world's biggest fake and actually a bitch of the first water, it didn't matter a bit, it didn't affect the perception at all, because the person who lived on the screen in *Scenes from a Marriage*—the woman named Marianne who fought her way to love and self-understanding in the most perfect way, without castrating, without giving up the old feminine ideals of tenderness and compassion and understanding—would live forever as a reality that could inspire.

What then truly catapulted Liv Ullmann into the

status of being some sort of 1975 superwoman was the dawning awareness, as interviews and stories created the real person, that this real person was totally like the role it had created. So the first perception was confirmed, and its confirmation brought reinforcement to it, so that it became even stronger as more enthusiasm was pumped into it, the enthusiasm of the discovery that one's instincts were, for once, quite correct, that no Hollywood gloss covered this film product, that "what you saw was what you got."

Enhancing the fascination of the perception was the one mystery connected with it: How much of all the torment and conflict between the couple in *Scenes from a Marriage* was a reflection of Liv's life with Ingmar Bergman, who after all, it could hardly be forgotten, was the creator of this screen masterpiece and therefore of its star. The speculation on this score was hardly necessary for the apprehension and enjoyment of the movie's qualities. It appeared almost unbidden in the mind of the viewer, and as it did so, it gave a further resonance to the scenes from a marriage they were watching on screen, an electric current that connected back to Liv's five years with the great director.

Leaving aside for the moment just how real that current was, we can move back to the surface of the film and of Liv's own reaction in order to understand how she was able to bring to the role the energy and conviction that jump from the screen. Her reaction to the film was one of total enthusiasm, in terms which mirrored precisely the audience's reaction to it. "It's so true to life," she says. "It just digs into the heart of everyone's problem, whether they are married or not, even whether or not it's a heterosexual relationship you're speaking about. You know, homosexuals have been absolutely bowled over by the film, and I can understand why, because at the most basic level, it's about getting along with someone, about communicating with them and having a relationship on real terms, not the artificial construction that so often pass for reality. It's a film that means something to everyone who sees it, because it comes right out of their own lives, and because it shows a way to move past this problem that everyone has, not the only way of course, but a possible way, and not a phony one either. After all, at the end of *Scenes*, you can't say that the couple are truly fulfilled in life—after all, they're each married to another person, although they feel that they truly love each other—and you can't even say that the imperfection they are finally willing to live with is all that marvelous. They still don't match each other one hundred percent. But that maybe is the most wonderful thing about Bergman's conception, the idea that 'matching' is maybe a totally artificial thing, that it's not really possible, and that all of the millions of people in the world, men as well as women, who believe the old Hollywood happy ending, who reverberate to perfume ads about 'forever' are simply living in a dream world, and a dream world that's incredibly destructive because it keeps them marching off to new songs. Every time the violins play, they're off again, saying to themselves, 'This is the one,' and of course it isn't. Or it is for a while, and then it's the same old funeral march, and that's the reason there are so many divorces.

"Now, in *Scenes*, in contrast, here are these two people who do get divorced, it's true, but that's the way society is, and yet they rise above that, they realize that there are these strong bonds between them still, and divorce is just a piece of paper compared to these bonds. And the point is, they *stay* with each other, not physically in the sense of living together, but physically and mentally, or spiritually if you want, in the sense of knowing that they belong to each other in some mysterious way and the point of life, the film says, not the only point, because there are careers and there are other things one can commit oneself to besides perfecting a personal relationship, but a point at least is for two people to adjust themselves to each other so that they can know *themselves* as well as they know the other person. Because after all, is there anything worse in life than desolate loneliness!

"Of course the film limits itself to this idea of perfecting a relationship because after all it's only one film and you have to limit it somehow. So maybe that makes it artificial in a sense, too narrow. But then again, it's a question of values. What do you want most out of life, a career or love and sharing with someone else. And anyway, the film does speak about careers, so it's not as if Bergman is saying it's one thing or the other. He's saying that this area of relationships is an important one, maybe the most important one, but anyway, here's how one couple are buffeted by it, and here's how they finally weather the storm—not perfectly, they're very much scarred, but the scar tissue is very strong and they've made it back to a safe port."

It is this perceptiveness that guides the brilliance and intensity with which Liv Ullmann plays Marianne in *Scenes from a Marriage.* And coming back to her audience's conception of her, it is this perceptiveness that confirms to them that she is truly what she seems to be. There is a strain of humanity, a genuine liking for people that rises above liking for self in all of this. That is perhaps why she is able to say that she welcomes the camera's probing eye, the lack of guilt about her own life which is rooted in a practical and idealistic concern for others as a way to perfect her own self. "I think we should dare to show what's inside of us," she says. "I think the problem with the world today is that we have masks."

Liv Ullmann tries not to hide from the world, and

this openness is apparent. In an interview she is so direct that often veterans of this slick trade are rendered unfunctioning. "Am I really hearing what I think I'm hearing?" they are forced to ask themselves. The answer is yes, and the reason goes to the heart of Liv Ullmann's outlook on life. She has thought about who she is, and she continues to do so, and she does it not in terms of herself as a movie star but in terms of herself as a person. Thinking about her alliance with Bergman, for example, she considered the difference between Norwegians and Swedes. "Really, deep down inside," she reflected, "we're all the same. But I think in many ways, the society of Sweden is more sophisticated, and the business more developed. And the moral freedom of Sweden is greater. The Swedes have been in the big world for a long time now. We're actually thirty years behind, though that's catching up, and in some parts the intolerance—of the church and so forth—is greater in Norway." All of this has obvious reference to her experience with Bergman and with Norwegian society. The Lutheran church in Norway, after all, refused to baptize her daughter.

She knows, too, how confusing modern life can be. Thinking of Nora in *A Doll's House* leaving her husband, she says, "We walk out the door and we're very unsure about where we are going and about what we are trying to find. That's the way my first marriage ended. It wasn't a bad marriage, but it was dull. Whatever safety you find, it has to be inside yourself. Then at least nobody can take it away from you."

And she sees correspondences to the complete world around her. She was horrified at Watergate and furious with Richard Nixon, yet not without compassion. "I start to feel sorry for Nixon," she says. And when the interviewer makes a face, she goes on quickly. "No, no, he was alone, too. He's like you inside, too. And it can't be very easy to be found out, and so publicly, and every day in every way. And it's your system. One should also maybe question the system and the method of election. In Norway we have changed governments often. We have had a Socialist one, a Christian one, a very conservative one, and now the Socialists are back again. And in a way it sounds very mixed up, but it's also very healthy because there's no time for corruption to set in. Why, we had one prime minister, very nice, a farmer who had to go just because he was on an airplane one time and he showed some papers to the man sitting next to him. They were secret papers—not so big a secret, but a secret all the same—and when it came out that he had done this, and they asked him about it, he said he didn't do it. He lied about the whole thing. Then ultimately it was proved that he had lied, so in the end he had to go, and that was right."

October 1974. Liv Ullmann is in new York to promote *Scenes from a Marriage*, and an interviewer goes to see her at the Hotel Pierre, which like the Plaza is on Fifth Avenue but, in place of the Plaza's studied busyness, preserves an atmosphere of palatial quietude in its lobby, with its decor of brass and marble coolness. In her room, Liv is watching a game show on television with a mixture of amazement and disbelief. She tells the interviewer that she is still recovering from the shock of an episode she saw just a few minutes before. Relating this, she is wonderfully animated and relaxed, the freckles on her nose bobbing as she speaks, occasionally her hand moving without self-consciousness to smooth her elegant halo of red-gold hair. "It was so awful," she says, "this poor woman and her poor husband. Why do people on television—the ordinary people—think they have to tell the whole, awful truth? They asked this woman what the worst thing about her marriage was, and she actually told them. 'It's our sex life,' she said. 'It's really terrible.' And then of course the camera switched to her husband in the audience, and he wanted to dive under his seat."

Her eyes still checking the set, and listening with half an ear to what was going on, she said, "The funny thing is the other side of the coin. The celebrities who are on all these shows and supposedly are being so honest are obviously not sincere at all; they're just trying to evade being their selves. Yesterday I saw Burt Reynolds on a show, and he was talking about what he'd like to do to the critics who didn't like his new movie. And he was so obviously playing a role. But of course he was charming. I think if someone famous went on one of those talk shows and was honest and sincere, he would look like a total fake. No one would believe him. That's a frightening thing to think about the world today. There are so many situations where being honest is exactly the wrong thing to do."

Stig Järrel (Caligula) and Alf Kjellin (Jan-Erik) in FRENZY.(1944) photo *Svensk Film.*

Liv Ullmann in Hollywood. With Edward Albert in FORTY CARATS. Photo *Pressens Bild.*

Liv Ullmann as queen Kristina in
THE ABDICATION.
Photo *Pressens Bild*.

In the leading part in POPE JOAN, a British film from 1972. Photo *Pressens Bild*.

As Nora in Ibsen's A DOLL S HOUSE with Sam
Waterston (Helmer) during a guest performance in
New York spring 1975. Photo *Pressens Bild*.

TIME

Hollywood's New Nordic Star

Liv
Ullmann

Liv Ullmann on the cover of Time in December 1972.
Photo *Pressens Bild*.

Liv Ullmann in a scene from the film, CRIES AND WHISPERS. Photo *Pressens Bild*.

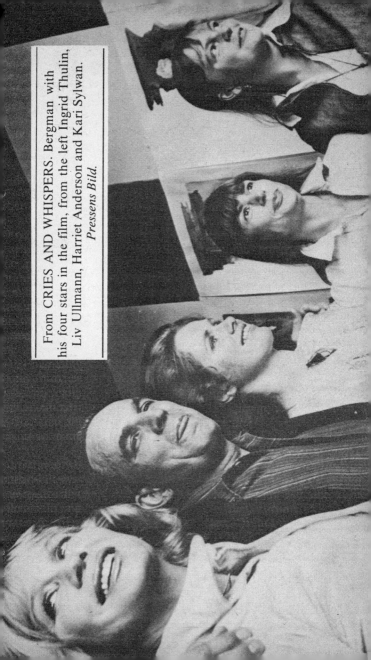

From CRIES AND WHISPERS. Bergman with his four stars in the film, from the left Ingrid Thulin, Liv Ullmann, Harriet Anderson and Kari Sylwan.
Pressens Bild.

Liv Ullmann and Erland Josephson as Eliza and Higgins in Shaw's PYGMALION at Maxim autumn 1975. Photo *Pressens Bild*.

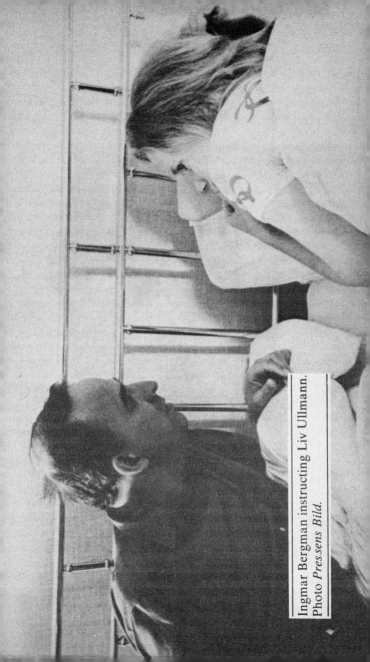

Ingmar Bergman instructing Liv Ullmann.
Photo *Pressens Bild.*

Liv Ullmann and Erland Josephson (Johan) in
SCENES FROM A MARRIAGE the TV series shown
as film abroad, becoming the big break-through to a
large international public for Ingmar Bergman as well
as Liv Ullmann. Photo *Pressens Bild*.

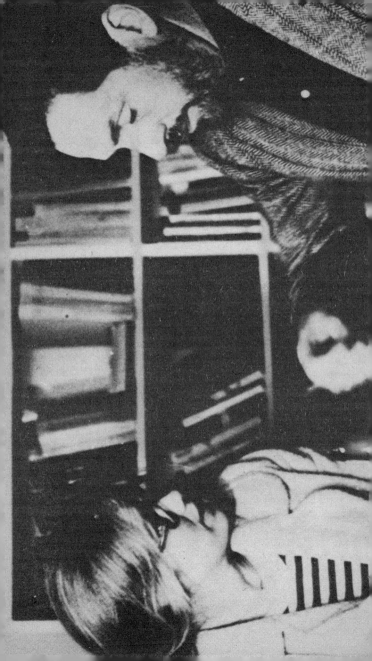

CHAPTER SEVEN

A Complex Woman

In Sweden, in Europe, they make more movies about women because they feel more interest in women's inner soul. On commercials in America, nobody talks about the inner side of women. They only do things to their outside, to their smell, their hands, their hair, for the husband when he comes home. That's their idea of attractiveness in a woman, while a man reads the newspapers or does other things. They've made a myth of the American woman everyone wants to get away from.

—Liv Ullman in a 1974 interview

Film gives Liv Ullmann a misty innocence. The camera catches and holds each expression in the fast-moving circle of feelings that rush across her face like wind across a field of hay.

In person, however, it is a kind of pioneer plainness that comes through. Tall, earthy, and pale-skinned, she stands forth as raw self—unadulterated by pastes, polishes, and powders; unadorned by the airs and attitudes that you might expect to find in one of the world's most acclaimed actresses.

She totally lacks that sense of urgent self-importance that many stars carry with them offstage or off camera. When she speaks in her lightly accented English, turning over each question in her mind even as she answers it, her voice is strong and resonant.

"I like to do plays and pictures that talk about real problems, about people being put on shelves and trying to get off them," she told an interviewer. "Especially in America, we have everybody telling us what to be—you shouldn't be a Communist, you should have blonde hair—and not many people know who they really are."

Liv Ullmann was in New York to do exactly the kind of play that concerns her. She would open on March 5, 1975, at Lincoln Center with Sam Waterston playing Helmer to her Nora in Henrik Ibsen's *A Doll's House*. This would be her first stage performance in English; playing a woman who breaks out of her hermetically sealed marriage to find out who she is. When Joseph Papp made a trip to Norway last year to coax her back to his New York Shakespeare Festival Theater, it was she who chose the play. She had been giving the farmers of Norway a glimpse of the flowering of Nora on a bus tour of the play that spring.

She thinks of herself as living whatever she acts, and in some ways, acting what she lives. It is all a part of the whole. Her last and highly successful Ingmar Bergman movie, *Scenes from a Marriage,* and *A Doll's House* are lined up with her own concerns and preoccupations about male-female relationships.

She likes to compare the marriage of Nora and Helmer in *A Doll's House* with the marriage of Johann and Marianne in *Scenes*.

"Marianne was the one who benefited from Johann's leaving, as though she, like Nora, had done the deserting," she said between bites of a roast beef sandwich. The scene had shifted, by taxi, from the hotel to the rehearsal space for the play, the Manhattan Theater Club on East 73rd Street. "It's often the one left with the disaster who pulls herself together and grows. Johann wanted to break out of his role also, but he only got halfway—going off with another woman, but still not being able to change his way of handling life."

Bergman, too, she noted, felt the similarities between his own creation and Ibsen's. In the original script, in fact, Johann and Marianne go to a production of *A Doll's House* and then argue about it. That portion was finally cut because Bergman thought it was too obvious and heavy-handed.

"Both couples never show who they really are to each other," she said. "Both are trying hard to play the part they think the other person wants them to play."

In both the play and the film, too, there can be the reference to Liv Ullmann's own experiences as the consort of Ingmar Bergman. Asked about this, she said, "I just think that sometimes it is less hard to wake up feeling lonely when you are alone than to wake up feeling lonely when you are with someone." The remark was, as are so many of her remarks, unerring in hitting the mark of a contemporary condition. In times past, when couples stayed together to a much greater degree than they do now, the luxury of this feeling might not be allowed. If it came unbidden, it would be stifled. Today with the institution of divorce and the current of alienation as strong as they are, it is not stifled but acted upon.

The pressure on a woman not to live alone is still great, and Liv Ullmann is aware of it—feels it strongly, in fact. Whenever she goes to a restaurant alone, she hides in a corner with a book so that no one will be able to stare at her. "Some women would be better off alone," she says, "but they feel that they've got to get a hold of someone to prove that they are worthwhile. If they do go on alone, part of their loneliness will come from an exaggeration of the feeling that something is missing from their lives, that society is somehow looking down on them because they are playing the wrong part, they haven't found a partner."

Liv Ullmann is willing to grant that these women ought to seek any kind of help they can get to adjust themselves to their situation—including psychiatric help. But she is adamant in her feeling that she herself would never go to see a psychiatrist. Working with Bergman, she feels, is the equivalent of psychiatry in many ways. "It's like being part of a psychodrama," she says. "We are lucky. He's the doctor, and all we need to do to take the cure is work in his films." In *Scenes,* she and Erland Josephson felt their way through the script, improvising at times, and at times reaching real heights of emotional catharsis. As she has said so often in the past, she marvels at the way Bergman is willing to give his actors the freedom to expand on his vision and "to accept what you are trying to do, even though he never imagined it that way himself."

In one scene, for example, Johann and Marianne are locked in his office. They have come there to sign divorce papers. They have made love in an easy, highly erotic way, lying on the floor. They have been planning to go out to dinner. But suddenly Johann becomes furious at something Marianne says. He locks the door and starts to beat her up. She fights back and he becomes even more ferocious, punching her, knocking her down, kicking her with enormous fury. Her face becomes bloody, his a mask of hate. It is a remarkable scene, acted with an intensity that is as strong as a hurricane, and yet with a certain coolness of observation that is Bergman's master directorial touch. This is no barroom brawl, it's a ballet of hate and violence, closely observed not so that the audience can get its perverse kicks from a bloodied woman, but as part of the anatomy of despair that Johan's and Marianne's noncommunication brings. And the outstanding reality of it is, of course, that this noncommunication surfaces at what should be the closest moment in a couple's life, just after they have made love.

"Erland did not want to beat me up," Liv says. "He argued with Bergman because it was not what he would have done himself in his private life. When he finally agreed, it really all came out and I was very glad I wasn't really down there receiving his kicks. He even surprised himself."

During that scene, too, Liv departed from the script in what was a surprise to her. "All of a sudden, after being beaten, I started flying out at him, hitting him. I just felt that it was important to show my panic and anger."

Like most women, Liv Ullmann said, she struggles against a deep, inbred feeling of guilt. She is trying to work this out of her life—in both films and plays as well as in reality—and parts like Marianne and Nora have, she feels, been an enormous help in this process. One aspect of her life that gives her "a bad conscience" is that she thinks she spends too much time away from her daughter. "That's because all of my life I have read in books that a mother should stay at home with her child. I try to convince myself that my daughter has received much more from me than she would have if I had stayed at home because my career is good for me as a person and as a woman. Yet it goes very deep, this guilt, and I always feel somewhere that I'm doing something wrong."

She illustrated this with a story of how the absurdities such feelings can generate cripple a person's impulse to action. "I had a dog that I loved for three years, and then I had Ingmar's baby. I felt so guilty I got a nanny for the child so that I would have more time for the dog. Then I found that I could have time for both, but I didn't have the heart to tell the nanny. I would be walking the dog and watching the nanny go by with the carriage, wishing I could take the baby out myself."

Being in America, Liv has become both hopeful and pessimistic about the status of women in the country. She sees the period as a transition time, with women reaching out for a new status and still reacting with confusion to the thought of what this status should be. That's why, she believes, there are no great American female film stars at the moment, with one or two exceptions. "It's not that there are not talented women in America," she says. "It's just that producers are not giving them the parts because the producers are not really sure how the audience wants women to appear in films—because it's still a little unsure how women want to appear in real life. Somehow the public no longer wants to see the sexpots because women have been knocked down from their pedestals, and that's good. But what we have in place of this—in films, at least—quite often is two men together. Maybe it's a fear of women's lib; maybe it's disguised homosexuality. Whatever it is, it's producing a vacuum—women are not being presented as human beings at this point—

and I suppose something will rush in to fill the vacuum, but I'm not sure what that something will be."

When word got around that Liv Ullmann was going to star in *A Doll's House,* the New York Theater-going audience reacted strongly, and Ibsen took on an unexpected box-office allure. The interest surrounding her American stage debut was such that the last tickets for the limited New York engagement were sold five days before the first out-of-town preview took place in Philadelphia. Meanwhile, the cast itself was in rehearsal, and as strong as Liv Ullmann's magic was on the audience, it was perhaps even stronger on those who were involved with her in the production.

Tormod Skagestad, director of the Norwegian State Theater in Oslo, had come to America to direct the play. He was quite concerned with the problem of doing the play in English after having done it in Norwegian. "It's a big problem for Liv," he said. "We have to 'wash out' the Norwegian cadence. It's very necessary to think in the language you act in, and if the Norwegian associations are not cut off, it's difficult to think in English."

Skagestad riffled through the pages of the marked script he was holding. "I think Liv has managed that beautifully," he said. "She is not a prima donna in any respect. Some actors don't like to be directed. They don't want to be criticised. She is very open to direction. She is such a fine artist with such a strong impact on the stage. There is a kind of light streaming out from her."

In the role, Liv seems very much of Ibsen's time. Her blonde hair is piled on top of her head, and she wears very little makeup. Barbara Colby, who plays Kristine Linde, Nora's childhood friend in the play, found this to be very disarming. "None of the things you expect from a star are there," she says. "You expect more affectation, you expect someone who is going to be less available. Her blue eyes are always right there. She listens like no other person I've ever known, both onstage and off."

This comment was echoed by Michael Granger, who plays Dr. Rank. "I've worked with Bogart, Anderson, Laughton. She's the only one who's ever looked me in the eye. I would say from past experience that I'm usually aware of the audience thirty or forty percent of the time. But working with Liv, I'd say that I'm almost totally impervious to the audience."

Liv herself was taking an intense pleasure in developing the role again for the American production. One thing she talked about was how she fleshed out the part. "Some actresses work by fantasizing details in the life of the character. I think the fun of acting is not to make fantasies but to depict something that is real, to ask oneself, 'What would a real woman do here and here?' The fun of it is building a character as if you were writing about a person. It is the closest you can come to writing if you are an actress—you write a person through your interpretation of her character and your actions onstage."

It was lunchtime, and Liv and the interviewer were seated across from each other at a table in a busy, cheerfully lighted restaurant not far from the Shakespeare Theater in Lincoln Center. "Your performance can't be based on emotions alone," Liv went on. "You might be fantastic one evening, but if it's all emotions and you don't really know what made you laugh or cry, how can you go back and do it again the next night? I must *know* what I want to do with Nora; I must sort of be standing behind her. Of course, it isn't all intellectual. Sometimes I start to feel, too—you see, the one doesn't contradict the other. But you must always begin by knowing what you are doing."

Liv is very enthusiastic about the technique and art of acting, and now she was delighted to explain just who she thought Nora was. "Nora, as she is, is faking a lot of the time. The audience must know it is looking at the fake and also be able to see that this is an actor showing off this kind of woman. That's the way we can have a dialogue: that's the way Ibsen can have a dialogue with the audience. He's telling them something and he wants them to react."

The waiter came to ask for the desert order and Liv smiled. "I really shouldn't, but they have a delicious mousse here, so I'll have it." She smiled again. "I love Nora as a character. She's more complex than some people realize. Her relationship with Dr. Rank is a good example. He talks to her about death all the time, you know, and she sort of likes it. Maybe she is very curious about such things—I mean, that's a side of her you can start to think about, a sign that she's not just a sweet little girl. She and Dr. Rank talk about sex, too, in a very disguised way. And she likes to have these talks. You can really find all these things in the play, and I think that's what makes Ibsen such a genius."

She returned to an earlier topic. "I said one shouldn't fantasize about the character, but there are some things one must think about. What did it mean in those days for a woman to go to a man to borrow money, as Nora does from Krogstad? It just wasn't done. So it is enormously extraordinary that she went to this man and borrowed some money. And still more extraordinary that she didn't tell anyone. Nora is an impulsive woman who ordinarily tells everything, so there must also be another dimension to her which enables her to keep such a secret. She didn't even tell her old friend Kristine how she got the money. She doesn't reveal her inner self; the real, good things inside her. That's the complexity of Nora's character. You could make her very strong from the beginning, but what's the play about then? Everybody would know she was going to be able to live without her husband.

"Part of her believes the little role she is playing and part of her doesn't. If she were comically pretending all the time to be his little squirrel, then she would be very, very bad. No, I think her actions also demonstrate her need to be loved and to be accepted. She never treads on anyone's toes. When Kristine tells her that she married her own husband because he was rich, Nora immediately says, 'Oh, I can understand that!' Of course, she *can't* understand that; she herself would never do it. She shows it later in the scene with Dr. Rank. But a remark like that shows the dualism in her: a woman who says something and means something else entirely. I think she's saying it to be nice and to stay friendly with Kristine. She says twice, 'Don't be angry with me.' She's so afraid, you see. Which makes her leaving home in the end an even greater thing.

"And I think Nora is quite a whole person because she does astonishingly high moral things. She is ready to get Dr. Rank to give her money, but when he tells her he loves her, she knows she couldn't sell herself for money. Very few women are that whole, in that sense. I think that is why Ibsen put that scene in the play, to show that this woman who is using and manipulating people, being sweet and lovely and all that, is a real, whole person."

Did she think Helmer was beyond redemption?

"No, I think Helmer gets his chance at last; Nora just gets hers earlier. Helmer is a victim of society, too. He had to do his part, and she didn't give him much of a chance to do something else because she was always playing up to his part. It was her responsibility as much as his. Helmer is as trapped as she is. Absolutely. Even more so, in a way, because her trap is a sweeter, more charming one. Everybody gets angry with him because his role in society isn't a very pretty one—and it's the same today. That's why we're so angry at men, not realizing that we given them their part to play as much as they gave us ours. It's we who have to change, not the men. They must make their change in themselves not for us but for themselves. Maybe if we change, they will change—not because they are threatened, but because they're getting whole new human beings to live with.

"But there is one scene in the play where I do fantasize. That's the scene where Nora leaves Helmer. I really feel that scene very personally. I do have pictures in my mind as I play that scene—Nora as a little girl, and with her father. Because she is saying good-bye to that. And she's not going out to find some other person to live with, to do this or do that. She's going out very insecurely to find herself. And that is not the usual reason for women leaving home. I mean, her fantastic freedom to go without knowing why the hell you're going. You just feel, 'I have to leave this stage of my life, I don't know for what. For myself, to be myself.'"

"We fell in love and we lived together. Ingmar divorced his wife and I left my husband. Sweden is very free, so I was not afraid of the scandal there, but Norway is a prudish country. I had been a married woman, and I belonged to a family where even the theater was not acceptable."

Liv Ullmann is talking about her life with Ingmar Bergman. It is the spring of 1972, two years since they parted. But the memories are still fresh. "Norway has a Protestant government. You must be Protestant unless you file a paper saying you want to be something else. I believe in God—not churches. I go to church for weddings sometimes, but I always feel the religious people that talk for God on earth do not quote him right. Religion should be an act of love, an alternative to politics. But there is no love spoken in the church—at least not in the Protestant church."

There is, obviously, a good deal of bitterness here. And no wonder. For Liv, in staying with Bergman, had simply followed the dictates of her heart and, in a highly moral sense, her conscience. If she did not love her husband, and she did love Ingmar, then it followed that she should not be with her husband and she should be with Ingmar. The fact that their child was born out of wedlock and before her divorce from Gappe Stang became final complicated the morality of the situation—at least in the conventional churchly and legal sense.

"It was very difficult for me," Liv says now, thinking back to seven years ago. "My mother was always fine about it, however, and I have also remained good friends with Gappe. He married again last year. And when I went with Ingmar, Gappe's mother wrote me a letter saying: 'When you married my son, I got a daughter. I still have that daughter.' She is a remarkable woman. My picture still hangs on her wall, along with those of her other sons' wives, and each Christmas she makes presents and sends them to Linn."

Now five years old, Linn is never too far from Liv's thoughts. "My happiest memory is that of my child being born," Liv says with a great smile. "I had always been afraid of having a child. I always thought I would be so terribly scared when the time came. But that night at the hospital—looking through the window and seeing the result of myself and someone I loved—was an incredible privilege. Ingmar was just as happy as I. He and his daughter are very close friends and they are always so happy when they are together. When I have other men in the house, Linn will say to me after they have gone, 'They are not so nice as my father.'"

Last year, Ingmar Bergman married again—for the fifth time. But even if Liv had remained with Bergman, they would not have married. "The only reason to get married," says Liv, "is to ask for God's blessing. I had done that once before, and I would feel silly doing it again. I am in love with somebody else now, but we are not thinking of getting married."

CHAPTER EIGHT

A Real-Life Soap Opera

It was very hard because there was a lot of dialogue to learn. We shot it in sequence, rehearsed for one week, then shot for a week. We couldn't have gone on much longer like that. There was no improvisation, almost for the first time with Bergman who lately is very free. We were not allowed to depart one word from the script. This was important because there was a lot of silly, banal talk. If we had been let loose, we would just swim out into sheer banality.

  —Liv Ullman talking about the shooting
  of *Scenes from a Marriage.*

Scenes from a Marriage is emotional dynamite. The normal response to a Bergman film is to be exhilarated by his artistic brilliance and overwhelmed by his insights into human suffering and yet, nearly always, to leave the theater feeling emotionally drained and depressed—especially after films like *The Silence, Shame*, and *Cries and Whispers. Scenes from a Marriage* makes a viewer feel a lot more hopeful about the human condition—more willing to accept the contradictions in the desires and actions of human beings, more willing to believe in the possibilities of growth and change, particularly for women.

The film presents Marianne (Liv Ullmann) and Johan (Erland Josephson) as a middle-class couple, in scenes spanning a ten-year period. At the start, they seem to be "a perfect couple," living in a comfortable home, proud of their two daughters, each with an interesting career, he as a psychology professor, she as a lawyer specializing in divorce cases. But as the film unfolds, we see that his show of vanity and arrogance masks a compelling insecurity and that her "contentment" masks a simmering anxiety and doubt. Their journey from false harmony to real discord is marked by a number of signposts: Their best friends quarrel bitterly in front of them. Marianne tries unsuccessfully to rebel against their parents' control over their lives. She faces a middle-aged client who describes the loveless marriage she hates, and Marianne must refer this to her own marriage. Johan is told by a colleague that the poetry he secretly writes is mediocre at best. In their one attempt to truly communicate, Marianne and Johan discuss their sexual problems, which are serious, but fail to face them squarely. All of these incidents portray a relationship that is on the verge of crumbling unless something is done to save it. Neither one is ready to make a move toward the other, and finally, Johan precipitates the breakup by running off with a young girl.

Marianne is laid low. She has consistently glossed over the problems in their marriage. Now, faced with Johan's actions, she is shocked, humiliated, distraught. She must somehow pick up the pieces, and when we see her a year later, it is obvious that she has begun to do so. For the first time since her marriage, perhaps in her life, she has truly been on her own. When Johan comes to visit her, she tells him of her lover, of her psychiatrist, reads to him from a diary she has been keeping which records with sharp honesty her feelings and reactions to life. Johan, on the other hand, is seen to be getting along worse. Paula, the girl he has run off with, is intensely jealous and keeps him on a short leash. Johan is already getting tired of his new situation. If there is a flaw in the movie, it occurs at this point, for, as Johan and Marianne have dinner together, as they spend an evening together and ultimately wind up in bed, it becomes obvious that they are still greatly drawn toward each other. Whether this current of feeling that pulls them together is love or something else, it is clearly present. Both feel it and respond to it. Yet neither speaks of it, neither makes a move toward reconciliation, and, as they part, we see that they will go on down separate paths—for a while at least. The decision not to try for reconciliation, unspoken as it is, seems rather arbitrary—the only weak spot in the film.

When we next see Johan and Marianne, they are in Johan's office, getting ready to sign divorce papers. Marianne has now grown greatly in her feelings of confidence and independence, and she exercises these feelings by seducing Johan, acting in a more sexually aggressive way than she has ever acted in their marriage. Immediately after making love, they vent their anger and rage at each other. Johan tells her how much he loathed her while they were married and then, finally, confesses that he didn't want the divorce. They have a bloody, violent fight, and then they sign the divorce papers.

In the film's final scene, which takes place some five years later, they have become lovers again. They meet in Stockholm while each of their spouses is out of town, and they go away for a weekend in the country. Each is the same person and yet a different person. Johan has come to terms with the reality that he has decided applies to him. He is far more humble; he has let the "little man" who's always lived within him become dominant; he no longer feels the need to present a swaggering, blustering image to the world to hide what he feels is his true insignificance. Marianne, on the other hand, is a figure of strength. Johan feels that in some way his life is behind him, his career will not blossom, he is not happy with the way things have gone for him, but he is reconciled to his destiny. Marianne looks forward with hope, she foresees new worlds to conquer, not large ones necessarily, but ones which will reinforce her feeling of having triumphed in her life. She is going uphill, Johan downhill. Yet they are bound to each other by their old life together, which is part—but only part—of their new selves. The other, greater and stronger part, is their new honesty with themselves and with each other.

So, each seeing the other clearly, as a cracked piece of china, glued together, Johan with far more cracks showing, they find that they are bound to each other by something stronger than anything that has happened, anything that has split them apart from each other. Is this something love? They speak about it, and Johan says that, in his imperfect way, he probably loves Marianne, and she loves him.

The themes and situations of *Scenes* are not new for Bergman. There is the same courageous exploitation of what lies behind the conventional masks, the social personalities of people, the same intensity of psychological encounters, the sudden outbursts of violence and rage, the same range of volatile emotions and shifting power dynamics that we have seen in such films as *Persona* and *Cries and Whispers*. Bergman's films have always had an extraordinary degree of psychological realism, but in the past it has almost always been expressed in a highly symbolic framework. In these films, ordinary reality merges into dream and fantasy, characters function as fragments of a single personality and often, the techniques of the film call attention to the film, which serves to break the dramatic illusion. In *Scenes*, these elements do not intrude on the psychological reality of the story being presented, and what emerges is a remarkable journey into the lives of people we recognize, can identify with and respond to. The acting performances of Liv Ullmann and Erland Josephson are so convincing, the dialogue so realistic, the conception of the relationship so subtle, that it is difficult to believe we are not eavesdropping on real people rather than witnessing a theatrical performance.

As in earlier films, Bergman relies heavily in *Scenes from a Marriage* on close-ups to explore the feelings of his characters. But in *Scenes*, he handles this technique much less self-consciously than usual; perhaps because the film was originally made for television and the technique therefore has a good reason for being used. The film belongs to a new genre of expanded psychological realism, in which complex modern relationships are explored. Focusing on two or three people, and achieving a depth of characterization previously thought possible only in novels, this new genre will undoubtedly be expanded, more than likely by Bergman himself, but also by other filmmakers.

An earlier example of this kind of film is Jean Eustache's *The Mother and the Whore*, which examines a complex triangle involving a childish, charming young man and the two women he is involved with—the independent young woman he lives with and the alcoholic, promiscuous nurse he takes as a second mistress. And some of John Cassavetes's films—notably, *A Woman under the Influence*—also can be included in this genre. Like Bergman, Cassavetes relies on the intense psychological encounter between individuals; and like Bergman, Cassavetes is a writer-director who is able to draw on his own emotional experience, using some of his intimate friends both as models for his characters in the writing and as actors in the final production. In both cases—Cassavetes and Bergman—the result is extraordinary emotional authenticity. When we see *Scenes from a Marriage*, we can't forget that Liv Ullmann and Bergman used to be lovers and must have drawn from this experience in the course of making the film.

In some ways, *Scenes from a Marriage* is related to the soap opera. The basic materials and subject matter are the same, although they are handled very differently. The connection was very apparent in *The Lie,* a teleplay written by Bergman but directed and produced by others in the United States, England, and Canada. Despite the fact that the production used very talented actors (the husband and wife were played by George Segal and Shirley Knight), the performances lacked authenticity, and as a result *The Lie* looked more like conventional soap opera than a Bergman movie. In *Scenes,* Bergman is working with the same kind of soap-opera material and he uses the soap opera's serial structure; yet he retains all of the power and depth he has displayed in his other films.

In *Scenes*, Marianne expands her power in a way that must be very appealing to women watching the film. And yet, *Scenes* has attracted an audience that includes men as well as women. The reason that men do not rebel against a film in which, in some ways at least, the dice are loaded against the man in question—Johan—is that Liv Ullmann's performance is so unthreatening. On reflection, a man might object that Johan is really presented as a rather cardboard, one-sided figure, more than a shade too insecure, a man who is left with no compensations in his personality; for his insecurity extends to his work as well as his relationship with Marianne, and we all know successful men who are basically insecure and untalented, besides a charge which cannot be leveled against Johan because, in loading the dice against him, we are left with no idea of how good a scientist he is, though we do know he writes bad poetry.

Still, if Bergman gives Marianne all the best of the deal, and makes Johan the weak kind of a man that women's lib dotes on, so, too, did Ibsen make Nora triumphant over Helmer (though that was a different age, the male viewer might say). And Bergman knows he has Ullmann to make this potentially unpleasant woman named Marianne a creature who, far from being unpleasant, is endowed with just the right mixture of confusion, doubt, and female stubbornness before she "finds" herself to make her appealing enough to have even the men in the audience root for her triumph. And, after she has become independent and far more sexy, just enough of appealing femininity to go with her newfound assurance to dispel the idea that she has become a man-hating women's libber.

When Johan visits Marianne in the fourth scene of the film, a year after their separation, they sit on the couch together and she tries to explain to him how she has been exploring her own feelings since he's left her. Reading from the journal her psychiatrist has asked her to keep, she reveals an awareness that she has played the role of the passive female dictated by the culture, that she has learned to dissemble and deny her

117

own sexuality, that she has no idea who she is or what she is capable of. As we listen to this moving speech, we see a series of still photos of Liv Ullmann. A blonde child is singled out from a class photo. We see her again, naked, then mischievous as she holds a cat by the tail. We watch this spirit disappear in awkward adolescence, and observe the young woman arranged in a series of stilted poses, trained to act out a variety of roles, culminating in the bridal portrait. We try to figure out what, if anything, these frozen images can tell us about Marianne's inner self.

Marianne is eager to hear Johan's response to what she has read him, but he has fallen asleep. As her consciousness has begun to awaken, his is being drugged into numbness—or so it seems at the moment. But Marianne's (and Ullmann's) saving grace, in this rather too-obvious vignette, is her humanity. Her smile at Johan when he awakens is not totally forgiving, but it is understanding and realistic, at the same time that it is, ironically, indulgent as well, forgiving something that many another woman, given the circumstances, would hardly feel forgiving about. It is hard to be indulgent when one's ego is involved. Marianne's response in this instance, as Ullmann plays her so skillfully, is typical of the character she creates for Marianne as Marianne achieves her independence and self-awareness. It is a character that may gloat over triumphs but is nevertheless not going to lose sight of the heartache that preceded these triumphs, and so conscience and compassion and understanding leaven the self-reliance and independence, and there is nothing half-baked or crusty about the new Marianne.

In the next scene, in Johan's office, the situation is reversed. This time Marianne is the seductive visitor who yawns as Johan delivers an identity speech. He is the one who offers the brandy and wants to return to the safety of the marriage. Yet his clinging is a lot more violent than Marianne's has been. In the final scene, Johan comments directly on the reversal: "We've discovered ourselves," he says. "One perceives his smallness, the other her greatness." And then, as he invites her to bed, he jokingly asks, "Can you possibly—I say *possibly*—ration your boundless female strength?" And yet, he is not quite sincere in his estimation of the relative stature they have achieved. He does not fully believe he is so small, she so big. There is an ironic tone that undercuts the words. And it is to Marianne's credit that she accepts this ironic estimate, sees the justice of it, for part of the film's texture and significance, is its irony, hardly a quality soap operas cultivate. There is the larger irony that, small as he may have grown, Johan is still the man that Marianne needs.

The primary distinction between *Scenes from a Marriage* and soap opera is the way it affects us emotionally. The film's impact is tremendous. Instead of leading us to forget about our own lives, and to get caught up vicariously in the intrigues of others, it throws us back on ourselves and our own experience. The events in the film—the friends of Johan and Marianne quarreling, the middle-aged woman and her loveless marriage, these signposts which Marianne and Johan have ignored, have in part at least, led them to their terrible trouble. The audience sees these signposts, too, and ignores them at its own risk.

The film begins to have an analytic effect on those who see it. It is too real to be ignored, too real not to be taken seriously; whereas soap opera is of course too fantastic to be regarded as anything except diversion, events that happen to other people; not us, soap opera events. And even if we know people whose lives have become as complicated as those of the characters in a soap opera, we are wont to say of their problems, "It's just like a soap opera"; that is, it's almost unreal, and, in effect, it could never happen to us. *Scenes from a Marriage* tells an audience that this could happen to us, and it makes this message totally believable.

Watching *Scenes*, we see Johan and Marianne experience a kind of growth that has never before been captured on film. The portrayal of their marriage is so complex, so subtle, so varied and multidimensional that it is bound to trigger personal associations for anyone who has been involved in a long-term relationship. It makes us think about our own ex-husbands, ex-wives, and ex-lovers, wondering if those relationships would have followed a similar course if only we had a similar capacity for growth and the courage and the energy to persist. It makes us consider where those relationships stopped, at what stage and for what reasons, and where we are now in our own process of growth.

It is, in short, a seminal and significant film. It implies that if we have the strength to take a relationship as far as it will go, to discard as many false masks as possible, to live through the outbursts of hatred and violence, to honestly confront our full range of feelings, we may discover an emotional capacity that is much deeper and richer than we expect. The message comes through loud and clear in the film, and one reason that it does, of course, is that it is not just Marianne's message, but Liv Ullmann's message as well.

From the middle of the 1960s, Ingmar Bergman has been less concerned with religion, guilt, doubt, and faith, and far more concerned about the hypocrisies and passions of sexual and domestic life. It is obvious that this change in Bergman's direction coincided fairly closely with his professional and personal association with Liv Ullmann.

If *Scenes from a Marriage* was nothing else, it would stand as a tribute to this great actress's art and to Bergman's understanding of it.

The contrast to what she does in *Scenes from a Marriage* is underlined by her appearances in *Lost Horizon* and *Forty Carats*, the first two films she made in Hollywood, in both of which her natural talents and beauty were overshadowed by Hollywood production values of various kinds. In contrast, her scene with Johan on the couch as she reads from her journal is a marvelous example of her acting skill. And beyond that, whether Bergman had this directly in mind or not, the speech she says is as much Liv Ullmann's as it is Marianne's: "Suddenly I turned around and looked at the picture of my old classmates, when I was ten. I seemed to be aware of something had been lying in readiness for a long time, but beyond my grasp. To my surprise, I have to admit *I don't know who I am* ... in the snug little world which Johan and I have lived so unconsciously, taking everything for granted, there is a cruelty and brutality implied which frightens me more and more when I think back on it. Outward security demands a high price: the acceptance of a continuous destruction of the personality."

This is as much Liv Ullmann speaking of her own life as it is Marianne speaking of hers. And in the images of Liv Ullmann's young face in the photographs, we see some of the qualities of passion, reticence, and charm which she has retained as a grown woman, and which we have already witnessed in the preceding sections of the film. (It is interesting to note that Ingmar Bergman took these photos of the young Liv to use in the picture without her knowledge—not that she would have objected to giving them to him—but when he introduced them on the set, she was quite surprised.) As this scene indicates, there is apparently no limit to her range as an actress: in the course of the film, we see her delineate a wonderfully varied panorama of moods: tenderness and respect for the woman who comes to her for advice on her marriage; a harrowing degree of shame and guilt when she learns that Johan is running off with another woman; proud and gentle sexuality during her first reunion with him a year later; calculated revenge when they meet in his office to arrange the divorce; and finally, gaiety, panic, and exhaustion in the closing section of the film, when they have become lovers once more.

It is not just the publicity releases and the stories in *Time* and *Newsweek* that are comparing Liv Ullmann to Garbo and Ingrid Bergman. Wherever *Scenes* has played in America and in Europe, there are dazzled and bemused filmgoers who, having seen Liv Ullmann in the film, are convinced that she is quite special in the pantheon of motion picture actresses. The popularity of *Scenes* is largely explainable by her presence, and the audience's gratitude for her being a particular kind of woman—a radiant, soothing Earth Mother who appears to heal the wounds that have been created by the current sexual enmity that comes out of women's lib. The woman she plays in *Scenes* is one who says that men and women are in this together, that the sooner this is recognized, the sooner we will see some kind of solution to the problem of the relationship between men and women, which may well be the largest and most perplexing problem of our time.

CHAPTER NINE

On Being a Woman

An artist can no more judge another artist than one child can judge other children. Each artist has his particular vision. You can't wear someone else's glasses. They would fit badly, and you wouldn't see. The artist's glasses work only when they are put on nonartists, whom they move, exalt, surprise. Of course, sometimes private and esoteric material becomes part of a more general discourse. It's clear that Joyce is appreciated by other artists because his vision of the world is marked by that neurosis, conflict and unhappiness which all artists share.

—Federico Fellini in Charles Thomas
Samuels, *Encountering Directors.*

She was in New York to do *A Doll's House,* and the reporter from *The New York Times* asked her about her current romances. There weren't any of consequence, Liv said. "Sometimes it is less hard to wake up feeling lonely when you are alone than wake up feeling lonely when you are with someone." The words struck a note of recognition in everyone who had ever awakened in the morning, glanced at the body lying next to them in bed, and inwardly groaned, "How did I ever end up with him (or her)?"

Liv was troubled that day. In addition to the normal anxieties of any theatrical tryout, she was—and is—made uncomfortable by her unique and lonely position in the theatrical firmament. For she is not just the best movie actress around these days, she is almost the only one. Streisand, Fonda, Redgrave, and the rest are character actresses beside her, angular and mod. Ullmann is also the only stage actress around just now who could sell out every seat in advance for a six-week run. The paradox of Liv Ullmann is that she is an entirely contemporary woman who satisfies everyone's nostalgic craving for an old-fashioned girl. Her quality is warm, clean, clear, friendly, and blooming. There is nobody else like her. Women and men flock equally around her. Homosexuals write to say that the progression of *Scenes from a Marriage* describes their relationships. Everybody wants to enlist behind her banners. She is a modern Joan of Arc who cannot quite hear her own voices.

Meaning something special to everybody, Liv Ullmann is not sure what she means to herself. She is full of doubts, guilts, and tremblings. Yet she is equally certain of the value of one thing: the importance of truth, openness, and vulnerability; of living in the moment. Like other great natural actors, she is continually subject to the idea that everyone else is acting—not acting onstage, but faking it in real life. Of Nora and her husband in *A Doll's House*, she says, "Both are guilty. Both are vulnerable. Both are victims.

But they don't know where they are hurting the other because they're never asking: 'Who is the other one?' Really, they're speaking to someone who doesn't exist. Somebody whom they have made up."

This is her one great advantage. Uncertain and doubting she may be about her own problems and actions, but she sees clearly into the hearts and minds of others. And the result is an extraordinary wisdom that cuts through the fog of motive to the clarity of effect, and, of course, this is one of the reasons she is so talented an actress.

Listen to her explain what happens to Nora after she walks out the door: "I don't think it's important. Whether she became a whore or a politician or whatever, it makes no difference. Because the important step was going out. When you do such a thing you never go back the same, even if you go back the next day."

But if she knows that it was right for Nora to move away from Halmer's bondage, to strike out on her own, she is not at all certain that the results of women's leap for self-reliance and independence has been an unmixed blessing. She is not all certain that the current sages of women's lib have discovered all the answers. Yet she knows, too, how passive women can be. "In some ways," she says, "I think women today have gone a step back. Because in those days, to try to get your freedom was such a big step that when you reached for it, it was something *you* had to do. Today we sit back and wait for it. We're very spoiled."

Liv does not like people who sit down. Liv is very stern, open, but naïve; childish, but full of folk wisdom. Onstage, her performance is all virtuosity, control, disciplined art. So one is not prepared for the disarming, wide-eyed creature one meets offstage. Milkmaid-pretty at times, a supremely sophisticated yet natural beauty at others, she is at heart a country girl who believes in discipline, hard work, self-reliance, and self-denial.

Although she was once married to a psychiatrist, she is dead set against that science. "I think we need our troubles," she says, "and we are the better for them. The important thing is not to arrive, but to be on your way." It is in good part because she has this attitude, because she presents to the public not the glossy, masklike face of a Hollywood cardboard figure whose dreams have come true and whose horizon is unclouded by a single cotton puff of worry, but the reality of a woman who has lived through some bad moments, is not afraid to speak of them and admits in all candor that she does not yet "have it all together," that she seems to the public eye to be a more beneficial symbol of women's liberation than the movement's official spokeswomen who can't help boiling the problem down to the man's side: as soon as men shape up, women will be in fine shape is the essence of their message.

Liv sees the problem as having a good deal more complexity than that. To begin with, she's noticed that American women are not above being "afraid" of Scandinavians and others with differing psyches and life-styles. "I don't know why American women are afraid of other women," she says, "Maybe it's because—to me, at least—American women seem like such bullies. They're so strong that they don't know how to control their strength. An American woman begins to drive the man very early. She exhausts him, and then she is displeased because he is so tired. American men are the most charming men in the world. They worship women. They are so polite. They still open the car door for you—not because they are gallant, but because they like you. They understand it's lovely to be courted."

Thinking for a moment, Liv ponders the reason why American women, with all their power, might fear females from across the sea. "Maybe," she says slowly, "it's because they're afraid of us sexually. But our sexual freedom is a myth. In Norway there is very little tolerance. And the Scandinavian man treats a woman like a friend. He is offhand—perhaps because he feels it is more sophisticated to be casual, to play at being friends. But then you must have sex to prove your intimacy with one another. Scandinavian women don't need to be courted. They are taught not to hold back."

Leaning back on the couch, she laughs suddenly. "I suppose an American woman might fear that; thinking that we're so easy men flock to us. But we've gotten beyond just the sexual thing, and I sometimes wonder if American women aren't still hung up on sex."

Asked why she feels that way, she replies, "I have the feeling that they're not really curious about themselves. Once they are in a relationship with a man, it becomes very static and status quo. As an actress, you become accustomed to having a director find in you something you didn't realize existed. That is also part of what it should be like for a woman with a man. I think women become very confused because they're living out the unconscious lives of their men. This is where women's lib really has meaning. An actress with a director has the unique chance of discovering herself—because she isn't stuck with the one role her man wants her to stick with."

There was a knock at the door, and when she called, "Come in," a waiter entered with coffee for us. After cups had been filled, she said, "A woman is taught to want to please so many people; a man to please only himself. I always feel like a cousin from the country. I feel so clumsy, so foolish, really. It took me a long time to realize that it's so foolish, so silly that we say to ourselves, 'I'm just a woman'.... Talent, even money don't count if you're a woman. Every woman has this complex, I think."

She is wearing a flowing dark brown silk dressing gown, and now she pulls her knees up to her chin and wraps her arms around her legs as she rests her chin on a knee. Her blue eyes are a little faraway. "I came to myself in a strange way, really. I started acting when I got out of high school. I acted only Shakespeare, Ibsen, Brecht. I seemed always to be a demented, drugged, a little crazy, a little sad. I didn't see myself in those parts. I was acting. But when I began to be with men, I started to understand. I'd never played a comedy part. I realized that there was a sad thing about me that men recognized and brought out. That was that, until I met Ingmar. He is very interested in women as human beings. Most men are show-offs to keep their distance with women, but he is very quiet and very deep. Even as a director, he hates to explain, to make rules, to chart the territory between people. He trusts that if something is there, it will come out creatively."

The reference was unmistakable. Not just a director working with an actress, but every man with a woman ought to have this attitude.

Once started talking about Bergman, Liv went on. "There is this extraordinary magnetism about him. He waits for you to give. He sees instantly. Bad directors see only what *they* would have done." There it was again, that encapsulated wisdom, in this case pinning to the wall with one on-target remark, the anatomy of bad direction forever.

"Ingmar knows the power of a relationship between two people; how it gives contrast, how it opens both people up. He has an absolutely amazing knowledge of human nature. He knows so much that, now when I look back to the roles I've played, I learn very valuable things for myself that I didn't even recognize then.

When I did *Persona,* I was twenty-seven. The actress I played was at the top of her career. She didn't want to change, to grow old, so she lost her voice. Because I didn't have the problem at the time, the whole thing seemed very foreign to me. Now I know what that part was about and why, internally, it was essential for me to have played it."

She sat up, stretched her legs in front of her, and stretched out her arms. "Ohh, I'm so tired," she said. "I didn't get enough sleep last night." Despite her fatigue, she was ready to talk some more.

"You see," she said, "I'm only now learning that the private life must be the most important. Being an actress and being a woman are always in conflict. I want to have my life as a woman, too. When I kiss a man, I want the bells to go off just as much as anyone else. When I was little, my mother would tell me men are so strong. But I know now that a man's strength is a false strength. Men need someone, too. This thing of strong and weak is so stupid. When I was eighteen, I was to be a virgin always. Where do we get these ideas? I was married at twenty. When I met Ingmar and got pregnant, I was still married. But I had begun to realize—marriage or no marriage—I was on my own. The only real safety in the world is the safety I feel in myself. I'm very privileged to have learned that."

"More coffee?" she asks, and when the interviewer says yes, she pours gracefully, and he wonders how she could ever feel clumsy, since she seems to have consummate physical control of herself. He tells her that and she giggles—a little girl's giggle.

"Isn't it all how we think of ourselves?" she asks rhetorically. "I don't think we know enough yet about the nature of women. I want to play all sorts of parts. I look at my daughter Linn, and I am astounded at how complicated she is, at just six. She calls every man who comes to the house 'Daddy.' She misses her father, but she also knows she has things to make up for that. She doesn't feel he has abandoned her. I don't want her to grow up with a lot of illusions that she'll have to get rid of later. I want her to know that life is not like that. Once she saw me crying because of a telephone call. It didn't frighten her. She left me alone. The grown-up world is not this big safe thing after all."

Her thoughts turn back again to *A Doll's House*; and she recalls the line of Helmer's. "No one would sacrifice honor for the sake of love," Helmer says, and Nora replies: "Millions of women have." This, she thinks, is one of the dividing lines between men and women. During a rehearsal, she asked her co-star, Sam Waterston, if he would give his profession away to follow some woman to a desert island. Waterston said he couldn't do that. Then Liv asked herself if she could follow a man. "And I said yes, I could. Many women could. Because we have some fantasy, or maybe real feeling, that love *is* more important."

Is that, the interviewer asked, because women put too low a value on what they do?

Liv was indignant. Her blue eyes blazed. "No," she said. "I think it's because we have a high value on what we *are*."